MW00325601

Moses, the Master, and the Manchild

EVERY 2,000 YEARS GOD HAS A SON

Moses, the Master, and the Manchild

Every 2,000 Years God Has a Son

Kelley Varner

© Copyright 2001 — Destiny Image Publishers

All rights reserved. This book is protected by the copyright laws of the United States of America. This book may not be copied or reprinted for commercial gain or profit. The use of short quotations or occasional page copying for personal or group study is permitted and encouraged. Permission will be granted upon request. Unless otherwise identified, Scripture quotations are from the King James Version of the Bible. Scriptures marked NIV, RSV, NAS, NKJ, TLB, and AMP are from the New International Version, Revised Standard Version, New American Standard, New King James, The Living Bible, and the Amplified Bible respectively. Emphasis within Scripture is the author's own. Please note that Destiny Image's publishing style capitalizes certain pronouns in Scripture that refer to the Father, Son, and Holy Spirit, and may differ from some Bible publishers' styles.

Hebrew and Greek definitions are taken from James Strong, *Strong's Exhasutive Concordance of the Bible* (Peabody, MA: Hendrickson Publishers, n.d.).

Take note that the name satan and related names are not capitalized. We choose not to acknowledge him, even to the point of violating grammatical rules.

Destiny Image₍ᵣ₎ Publishers, Inc.
P.O. Box 310
Shippensburg, PA 17257-0310

"We Publish the Prophets"

ISBN 0-7684-2121-7

For Worldwide Distribution
Printed in the U.S.A.

This book and all other Destiny Image, Revival Press, MercyPlace, Fresh Bread, Destiny Image Fiction, and Treasure House books are available at Christian bookstores and distributors worldwide.

For a U.S. bookstore nearest you, call **1-800-722-6774**.
For more information on foreign distributors, call **717-532-3040**.
Or reach us on the Internet: **www.reapernet.com**

Dedication

Rev. 1:9, KJV

I John, who also am your brother, and companion in tribulation, and in the kingdom and patience of Jesus Christ, was in the isle that is called Patmos, for the word of God, and for the testimony of Jesus Christ.

The Lord has commissioned me to strengthen those pioneering men and women who have been impregnated with divine purpose and who presently carry the prophetic burden of the Lord.

My brothers and sisters, we have already tasted and seen unprecedented "tribulation" or "pressure," the birth pangs of our divine, corporate destiny. Like John the Beloved, we have been separated unto the Kingdom and the patient endurance of Jesus Christ. Each of us has been apprehended and exiled by the predetermined pleasure of the Lord to his or her own "Patmos," literally, the place of "my killing." This is the cross we now bear in His name.

In this life, we have few close friends. I lovingly dedicate this volume to one of my elders, a classy lady, a mother in Israel, my sister in the Lord. Next to my wife, Joann, she knows more about me than anyone, yet she has remained constant in unconditional love and support. As a silver trumpet in the hand of the Lord, she has inspired and taught me how to effectively activate the corporate anointing in the lives and ministries of those to whom I speak. As an anointed psalmist and skilled musician, she has shown me how to boldly move in the Song of the Lord.

To Prophetess Clarice Fluitt of Monroe, Louisiana, I give honor to whom honor is due. I am your brother and companion in tribulation. I salute you and George, your lifelong partner and apostle of the Lord. "Momma Eagle," I love you.

Note: On Sunday morning, February 18, 2001, Clarice Fluitt ministered in our local church. When asked to pray over this submitted manuscript, she began to prophesy and sing the Song of the Lord. Her anointed words are recorded in Appendix A.

Acknowledgments

To my friend and publisher, Don Nori, for his initial witness and confirmation in the Holy Ghost for me to write this word from the Lord, and for writing its Foreword.

To my prophetic colleague, Don Milam, for helping me to clearly express the application of this book's message in Chapter Five.

To Des Short and the anointed campus community of Faith Bible College, Tauranga, New Zealand, where most of this book was written. His kind words are in its Preface.

To all those who are pregnant with the present purposes of God, who with me carry the prophetic burden of the Lord.

To the Holy Spirit, who is my Teacher.

Table of Contents

Foreword

Preface

Introduction

Chapter One   My Three Sons   1

Chapter Two   The First Son: Moses   7

Chapter Three The Second Son: The Master.   29

Chapter Four   The Third Son: The Manchild, the Mature Church   55

Chapter Five   Sing, O Barren   91

               Endnotes. 111

               Appendix A. 117

               Books & Tapes by Kelley Varner. 119

Foreword

Kelley Varner is a precious friend, a passionate writer, and a prophetic voice to this generation. You cannot read his books without being overwhelmed by the intensity of his insights into the prophetic purposes of the Lord.

Each new book he writes proceeds to erase the defective images created by traditional theology, replacing them with pristine pictures of compelling prophetic truth. It is my joy as his friend and publisher to add *Moses, the Master, and the Manchild* to the list of the books that Kelley has published with Destiny Image.

In this new book Kelley will take you on a 6,000 years' journey, exploring the three seeds of promise buried in the bed of humanity. They are sons of promise, predetermined by the foreknowledge of God to be revealed out of eternity into the time/space world of man. They are Moses, the Master, and the Manchild, God's corporate Man.

Kelley introduces essential prophetic keys that will help you unlock the mysteries of the ages. Those keys are found in the stories of these three main characters. The similarities in the experiences of these three sons are astonishing and will bring you great encouragement. Take a walk with Kelley as he leads you through the Scriptures into inspiring new vistas of fresh spiritual discoveries.

These discoveries will take you through the Tabernacle of Moses, straight ahead into the place of His presence—the Most Holy Place. Kelley and I have both shared a deep personal passion to remove all the obstacles that keep people from entering into that secret place.

As usual, Kelley pulls out his spiritual sledge hammer and pounds away at the misconceptions and barriers. In the end all you can see is Christ sitting in His rightful place, with outstretched arms, calling us to come on in without fear or shame. We *can* enter in, Kelley says, because we are a part of the story. We are the Manchild, the corporate Son called to reign with Him now and at the end of all time.

Don Nori, Publisher
Destiny Image Publishers

Preface

From the time of our first contact 20 years ago, Kelley Varner has impressed me as a man of God with faith and courage to venture where others would not dare. I see him as a modern Simeon, a man in the temple who hears from God and who cradles in his arms an infant who will one day become a mature son. This writing will instruct and inspire everyone who reads it, and will especially encourage those who are carrying the prophetic burden of the Lord.

The 21st Century Church is deeply indebted to this pioneer trailblazer and apostolic scribe who teaches and writes with great zeal and abandon. He is totally consumed with a vision from God and the strong desire to see its fulfillment. This profound message will provoke you to honor God in a way that will revolutionize your life.

This masterful writing is very practical for the new millennium Church, and is filled with insight, explanation, and revelation. I heartily recommend it to everyone who has divine destiny in view. Every minister should read and study this cutting-edge presentation.

This volume unlocks a fresh God-originating and God-glorifying perspective that will surely strengthen and sustain the human spirit for real fruitfulness even amid serious adversity. It is a book of power, beauty, and grandeur. Like a majestic symphony, it presents a royal rendition of the foreordained purpose of our awesome God in having a son every 2,000 years. There has never been another book quite like this one!

An understanding of the truth set before you is essential for any serious student of the Scriptures. Kelley Varner expertly unfolds the divine mysteries of the Kingdom in this priceless discourse. Armed with clear, uncommon vision, and a wealthy command of both the Old and the New Testaments, he slowly and systematically takes us through this amazing word from the Lord, opening the eyes of our understanding in a new, fresh, and insightful way.

For the one who longs to be part of this third Son, the mature Church, there is contained within the pages of this thought-provoking study a precious hope and assurance. In spite of sufferings, affliction, and trouble, we remain focused upon God's unchanging, unfailing, and unconquerable love.

You are on the brink of a magnificent and uplifting experience. Consider the steadfastness of God's grace that has been displayed through the life and ministry of the writer. Kelley Varner is a teacher who makes both the beauty and the truth of God's Word live with color and creativity. The brilliance in his writing is more than the product of human intellect alone. You are stepping into the pages of a script that was born out of travail as well as the fruitful experience of many, many years.

It is my pleasure to introduce you to a book that deserves to be a text for every Bible student, and a tool in the hands of every Christian. As the horizon of this truth expands before you, you will be captivated by its vision. As you continue to think on these things, you will be imprinted with the grandness of this prophetic treatise.

Kelley wrote most of *Moses, the Master, and the Manchild* while ministering for ten days on the campus of Faith Bible College here in New Zealand. Reading his original manuscript has been both a searching and uplifting exercise for me. I commend it to you with the prayerful expectation that its journey will be the same with you.

Des Short, D.D.
Principal
Faith Bible College
Tauranga, New Zealand

Introduction

I have been a Christian almost 35 years. The Lord Jesus sovereignly apprehended me on Friday evening, May 12, 1966. He filled me with the Holy Ghost two years later as I lay prostrate on the hard, wooden floor of the old Shaw Mansion in Barton, Maryland. From 8:00 p.m. until 1:00 a.m., I supernaturally spoke with other tongues, preached, and prophesied as the Holy Ghost turned me into "another man" (1 Sam. 10:6). Through the ministry of Pastors C. S. and Katherine Fowler from Berkeley Springs, West Virginia, the Lord subsequently introduced me to the faith walk and called me to preach the gospel of the Kingdom in 1969. From those small beginnings, I have painstakingly proclaimed His Word full time for over 30 years (the last 23 here on the Crystal Coast of southeastern North Carolina).

Hosea 6:1-3, KJV

Come, and let us return unto the Lord: for He hath torn, and He will heal us; He hath smitten, and He will bind us up.

After two days will He revive us: in the third day He will raise us up, and we shall live in His sight.

Then shall we know, if we follow on to know the Lord: His going forth is prepared as the morning; and He shall come unto us as the rain, as the latter and former rain unto the earth.

2 Pet. 3:8, KJV

But, beloved, be not ignorant of this one thing, that one day is with the Lord as a thousand years, and a thousand years as one day.

The year 2000...

The mere mention of that pivotal date seems strange and wonderful. Traditional eschatology has had to repeatedly rearrange its faulty predictions to accommodate the arrival of this "third day" from the days of Jesus' earthly ministry. The 21st century is dawning, and we are still here! Between His departure and His return, the King's instruction and admonition to His disciples remain unchangingly clear: "Occupy [do business] till I come" (Lk. 19:13, KJV).

We have been preserved and "kept by the power of God through [His] faith for [full] salvation ready to be revealed in the last time" (1 Pet. 1:5, NKJ). The Living Bible adds that God "will make sure that you get there safely to receive it because you are trusting Him. It will be yours in that coming last day for all to see."

The Lord has brought His faithful remnant out of Egypt and through the wilderness. He now stands postured to bring us, His army, across the Jordan River into the land of our inheritance and promised portion (Deut. 6:23). The Captain of the Lord's hosts stands in our midst with His sword drawn, His Word revealed (Josh. 5:13-15). He has gone before us, and will "without fail" drive out our every enemy and obstacle (Josh. 3:10).

We have been purchased by His blood and purposed by His Word and Spirit. Jesus has freed us from the tyranny of worldliness and sin, filled us with hope and power throughout our journey, and now patiently waits to fulfill His predetermined plan in every life. Our noses are pressed hard up against the glass as we look forward to our individual and corporate destinies.

Jer. 23:33, KJV

And when this people, or the prophet, or a priest, shall ask thee, saying, What is the burden of the Lord?...

Mal. 1:1, KJV

The burden of the word of the Lord to Israel by Malachi.

The prophets of the Old Testament, especially Isaiah, carried the "burden" of the Lord.[1] This is the word *massa'*, and it means, "a load or burden; figuratively, an utterance or oracle." It is derived from a Hebrew verb which means, "to lift." *Massa'* is translated in the King James Version of Proverbs 30:1 as "prophecy."

The message of this book is particularly sent to you who bear the prophetic burden of the Lord's present purposes for the nations of the earth. I cannot speak for any other preacher or Christian, but the year 2000 was one of my best/worst years. The "burning fiery furnace" was heated seven times hotter (Dan. 3:6,19). Close associates and peer ministries have concurred when asked, "How was the year 2000 in your life?" "It was really hard...tough...trying...," they responded.

Like you, I need some real answers. Like you, I have been seeking the Lord. When God whispered the following phrase into my ear, the Holy Ghost leaped in my spirit! The Lord said, "Tell My people that every 2,000 years, I have a son..."

First, there was Moses...

Second, there was Jesus, the Master...

Third, there is now His overcoming Church, the Manchild...

Set before you is the prophetic paradigm of God's three sons. This model will explain why the journey has not been easy, and why the weight of our burden and calling seems greater than ever before. In each of these three examples, we will unveil this continuity of truth:

1. The Person — God's chosen deliverer.

2. The Persecution — God's chosen adversary.

3. The Passover — God's chosen season.

4. The Provision — God's chosen transfer of wealth (health and blessing).

Mt. 24:8, KJV

All these are the beginning of sorrows.

Mt. 24:8, NAS

But all these things are {merely} the beginning of birth pangs.

Rejoice, brethren! Every 2,000 years, God has a "son." The season of birthing the divine Seed has begun. The Sun of righteousness is arising with healing in His wings (rays) in the dawning of this new day (Mal. 4:2). He is stretching the "womb of the morning" (Ps. 110:3) by the increase and enlarging of Himself within a people.

It was providential that most of *Moses, the Master, and the Manchild* was written (from September 27 to October 6, 2000) on the campus of Faith Bible College, Tauranga, New Zealand. Nearby, on the same East Coast of North Island, lies the city of Gisborne, the first city on this planet that literally sees the sun of each new day. Gisborne, New Zealand, was the first place in the earth to witness the year 2000—the first city to behold the dawning of this new decade, this new century, and this new millennium!

Gal. 6:9, KJV

And let us not be weary in well doing: for in due season we shall reap, if we faint not.

Lk. 18:1, KJV

And He spake a parable unto them to this end, that men ought always to pray, and not to faint.

Someone has said, "It is time to P-U-S-H—Pray until something happens!" We who co-labor with the Lord are bent over with the birth pangs of manifesting His predestined will and plan, until Christ be formed in a people, His third "son."

The saviors that are arising on Mount Zion are all reconcilers, peacemakers, and medicine men. The enemy has raged, yet the nations and their wealth are beginning to come into the house of the Lord. The Year of Jubilee's release is upon us. You and I have come too far. The Lord has kept us. His anointing has brought us out and brought us through. His third anointing of "fresh oil" now brings us in (Ps. 92:10). This is not the time to faint. This is our long awaited due season. This is the time to push!

Pastor Kelley Varner
Praise Tabernacle
Richlands, North Carolina

Chapter One

My Three Sons

About every 2,000 years, God has a "son"...

This holy seed is thrice revealed in the eternal Word, each predestined to be manifested in the history of a time/space world as His chosen deliverer—a savior, a mediator, and a reconciler.

Centuries before the birth of Jesus, Jehovah raised up the stuttering shepherd Moses, the adopted prince of Mizraim, the mediator of the Law, to rescue His people from Egyptian bondage and Pharaoh's cruel oppression.[1]

Nearly two thousand years later, the heavenly Father sent the Prophet like unto Moses, humankind's only Savior, the Word made flesh, the one Mediator between God and men and women—the Lord Jesus Christ.[2] His death, burial, resurrection, ascension, and coronation set us all free from the power of sin and satan.

Two thousand years, two prophetic days, have marched by since Jesus of Nazareth walked along the sandy shores of Galilee and down through the winding, unpaved streets of old Jerusalem. The time has come for God to bring forth a glorious, overcoming Church—His corporate Heir—commissioned with the same anointed word and ministry of reconciliation.[3] The unveiling of these sons and daughters as they roar out of Zion will bear witness to Jesus' once-for-all triumph, and will rid the earth of the influence of satan and the residuals of the curse.

Jehovah's first son was Moses, the intermediary of the Law, which was carved upon tables of stone. His second Son was the Pattern Son Jesus, the arbiter of grace and truth, which is written upon the hearts of men and women by the Holy Spirit. The Father's third Son is a corporate entity, the glorious Church, His many-membered Body and ongoing Messianic incarnation, called forth to administrate His law out of Zion, and to execute His Word throughout the nations.

In the Old Testament, the marriage covenant between Jehovah God and the nation of Israel produced a Son—the Messiah, the Heir of all things, the Word made flesh, who was made of a woman, made under the law.[4]

In the New Testament, God (Jesus) married the Church and from that covenantal *intimate* union is about to bring forth a corporate Manchild, a mature people, an overcoming remnant.[5]

Obad. 1:21, KJV

And saviours shall come up on mount Zion to judge the mount of Esau; and the kingdom shall be the Lord's.

2 Cor. 5:18,20, KJV

And all things are of God, who hath reconciled us to Himself by Jesus Christ, and hath given to us the ministry of reconciliation;

Now then we are ambassadors [elders, mature ones] *for Christ, as though God did beseech you by us: we pray you in Christ's stead, be ye reconciled to God.*

Rev. 21:7, KJV

He that overcometh shall inherit all things; and I will be his God, and he shall be My son.

All three "sons" encounter a fierce adversary. Jehovah allowed Moses to face the wrath of Pharaoh, whose soldiers murdered and drowned the newborn Hebrew males (Ex. 1:15-22). Early on, Jesus was spared from the jealous rage of Herod the Great, who butchered the babies of Bethlehem until Rachel wept (Mt. 2:16-18). The "man child," the mature Church, is presently staring down the global demonic strategy of the "the great red dragon" whose devilish intent is to assassinate and abort the godly Seed (Rev. 12:1-5).

Pharaoh tried to kill the first son, who was born to Amram and Jochebed. Eventually, the Red Sea swallowed up Egypt's king and his army. In that same Passover season of deliverance, Moses' "church in the wilderness" (Acts 7:38) bankrupted the land of the Nile. The descendants of Abraham received over four hundred years of back wages as a nation was born in a day.

Herod attempted in vain to destroy the second Son, the Pattern Son, and consequently died under the judgment of God. Jesus Christ finished the work that the Father had given Him to do. His death on Calvary's cross rent the veil from the top to the bottom, releasing everything that had been hidden for ages and generations. Jesus, the Seed of both Abraham and David, became the Heir of all things in Heaven, in earth, and under the earth. All spiritual blessings are His to own and dispense, supplying every human need.[6] He inherited the "land" and the "throne," the earth and the right to rule it!

The great red dragon is presently aiming to exterminate the third Son, the many-membered Body of Christ, but his best efforts have proven futile. The devil has already given the elect his best shot, and failed! He has been defeated! The forces of the Gentiles, the wealth of the nations, the glory and honor of the kings of the earth, have already begun to flow into His glorious Church, the House of the Lord.[7]

Heb. 11:28, KJV

> *Through faith he* [Moses] *kept the passover, and the sprinkling of blood, lest he that destroyed the firstborn should touch them.*

The Passover paradigm permeates our whole model. Moses, the first son, by faith inaugurated and kept the Passover, which is explained in detail throughout Exodus chapter 12. When God got ready to bring a nation out of bondage, He put a lamb in every house.

1 Cor. 5:7, KJV

Purge out therefore the old leaven, that ye may be a new lump, as ye are unleavened. For even Christ our passover is sacrificed for us.

Our Master, the second Son, *is* the Passover Lamb that took away the sin of the world by faith. Jesus delivered the whole creation from futility and corruption, then ascended up into Heaven so that He might fill all things with Himself.[8]

Heb. 6:4-5, KJV

...those who...have tasted of the heavenly gift, and were made partakers of the Holy Ghost,

And have tasted the good word of God, and the powers of the world [age] *to come.*

The Manchild, the mature Church, the corporate third Son, is about to enjoy the full benefits of the Passover of the Kingdom as we pass over into another age. This company of overcomers complete the trilogy of God's three "sons"—the mature Church will "sing the song of Moses the servant of God, and the song of the Lamb" (Rev. 15:3a)!

This is an epochal period, a *kairos* moment ("a fixed and definitive time"), an opportune season. The apostle Paul called this "the dispensation of the fulness of times" during which God would "gather together [sum up] in one all things in Christ, both which are in heaven, and which are on earth; even in Him" (Eph. 1:10). By faith, we have eaten the Lamb. We are the Lamb's kin.

The Lord stewarded my heart and hand with this assignment, "For this and generations to come, write down the story of My three sons!"

God's purposes always unfold in cyclical seasons of "excellent" or "threefold" things (Prov. 22:20). One primary example of this is the divine "pattern" of Moses' Tabernacle with its Outer Court, Holy Place, and Most Holy Place (Ex. 25:40). Another is the overview of the three primary Feasts of Jehovah—Passover, Pentecost, and Tabernacles (Deut. 16:16). The second chapter of my book *Prevail: A Handbook for the Overcomer* (Shippensburg, PA: Destiny Image, 1982, pp. 84-85) lists dozens of examples of these "threefold" things. God always works in threes.

Every 2,000 years, God has a "son"...

The year 2000 and the dawning of the 21st Century have arrived. The time for the birthing and presentation of the third Son has come. The Bible describes this epochal season as the manifestation or unveiling of *the* Son in a company of people who have been conformed to His image and likeness.[9] The new millennium has begun. We who have been apprehended by His mercy and grace are sensing the "birth pangs" of an unprecedented prophetic burden. Our journey has been marked by great travail, which seems to be intensifying.

Every 2,000 years, God has a "son." This chosen one is a deliverer, a savior, a mediator, and a reconciler. Every 2,000 years, all hell breaks loose in the earth. Every 2,000 years, the dynamic of God's Passover is revealed, releasing God's people from fleshly bondage and satanic tyranny into the abundance of an unlimited provision, a massive transfer of health and wealth.

It's that time again in the earth...

Come walk with me through the Word of the Lord. God's first "son" of destiny was the prince of Egypt, a man by the name of Moses.

Chapter Two

The First Son: Moses

Every 2,000 years, God has a "son"...

The first son was Jehovah's mouthpiece unto Israel and a god unto Pharaoh. His second Son was Jesus, the Word made flesh, the Prophet like unto Moses. The Father is about to consummate His prophetic cycle in the earth by the unveiling of His third Son—the mature Church, recreated in the image and likeness of their Elder Brother.

Every 2,000 years, there is enormous opposition to the divine plan as God works in and through His chosen ones. Pharaoh hardened his heart against the word of Moses. King Herod furiously boiled over and ordered his henchmen to kill the baby Jesus. Rampant global ignorance of satan's defeat at Calvary's cross has allowed the ancient serpent to become a great red dragon. His venomous fangs have tried to fasten themselves onto the lives and ministries of God's elect, especially His apostles and prophets (Acts 28:1-6).

Every 2,000 years, God's people experience the seasonal deliverance of Passover that subsequently releases the blessings of unparalleled health and wealth.

We begin our story first with Moses, who was opportunely drawn from the river of doom, and reared in the house of Egypt's god and king.

The Person—God's Chosen Deliverer

Moses, whose name means "drawn or pulled out of the water," was handpicked by Jehovah to liberate Israel. Born to powerful Amram and conceived by his wise mother Jochebed, Moses possessed a Levitical heritage that would one day empower him to ascend the top of the mountain as the anointed priest of Yahweh. In the historical Psalms, Moses is called the sent "servant" and "chosen" of the Lord.[1] His life is highlighted in the biblical "Hall of Fame," Hebrews chapter 11, where he is listed among the mighty men and women of faith.

Heb 11:23-29, NIV

By faith Moses' parents hid him for three months after he was born, because they saw he was no ordinary child, and they were not afraid of the king's edict.

By faith Moses, when he had grown up, refused to be known as the son of Pharaoh's daughter.

He chose to be mistreated along with the people of God rather than to enjoy the pleasures of sin for a short time.

He regarded disgrace for the sake of Christ as of greater value than the treasures of Egypt, because he was looking ahead to his reward.

By faith he left Egypt, not fearing the king's anger; he persevered because he saw Him who is invisible.

By faith he kept the Passover and the sprinkling of blood, so that the destroyer of the firstborn would not touch the firstborn of Israel.

By faith the people passed through the Red Sea as on dry land; but when the Egyptians tried to do so, they were drowned.[2]

Moses' portion was the life of faith, instilled early in him by believing parents. They shrewdly hid him among the rushes of the Nile River, the very place where the Hebrew babies were being drowned by the king of Egypt. This "sink-or-swim" kind of faith would bear Moses up into the hands of his God, and safely carry him throughout the rest of his remarkable life and ministry.

Ex. 3:10, KJV

Come now therefore, and I will send thee unto Pharaoh, that thou mayest bring forth My people the children of Israel out of Egypt.

Micah 6:4, NAS

Indeed, I brought you up from the land of Egypt and ransomed you from the house of slavery, and I sent before you Moses, Aaron and Miriam.

Moses was Israel's chosen deliverer and savior. At the youthful age of 40, he zealously killed the Egyptian, much as Saul of Tarsus would later persecute the early New Testament Church.[3] Thus his first attempt to rescue God's people was carried out in the vanity of self-effort and self-reliance. His motive was right, but he was too conscious of men. Yet God would prepare an instrument of phenomenal success from these ashen circumstances of dismal failure. The One whose finger would carve the Law into Sinai's stone was fully cognizant that Moses' failure was due to a broken focus. Moreover, Yahweh foreknew that these human limitations would never constitute a legitimate excuse for His servant's disobedience.

Acts 7:20-22, KJV

In which time Moses was born, and was exceeding fair, and nourished up in his father's house three months:

And when he was cast out, Pharaoh's daughter took him up, and nourished him for her own son.

And Moses was learned in all the wisdom of the Egyptians, and was mighty in words and in deeds.

Acts 7:22, NIV

Moses was educated in all the wisdom of the Egyptians and was powerful in speech and action.

Moses was no ordinary child. The Living Bible of this latter verse says that he "became a mighty prince and orator." Moses was somebody, but God's sovereign plan would lead His chosen through the desert for 40 years, to learn the ways of the wilderness. All the wisdom and knowledge acquired in Egypt's institutes of learning was hardly adequate to make him ready for his divine assignment. He would need new credentials.

This "somebody" had to become a nobody, left to be tossed about in the throes of lonely desolation. God's man or woman must be drained of all self-sufficiency, molded in obscurity with the kind of meekness that refuses to shrink back from future publicity and scrutiny. Listen to the renewed attitude of this powerful preacher as he stands stripped in the presence of his Maker.

Ex. 4:10, NIV

Moses said to the Lord, "O Lord, I have never been eloquent, neither in the past nor since You have spoken to Your servant. I am slow of speech and tongue."

Ex. 4:10, TLB

But Moses pleaded, "O Lord, I'm just not a good speaker. I never have been, and I'm not now…"

Only through divine discipline could the rod of Moses ever become the "rod of God." Through this necessary processing, Moses, the "somebody" who had become a nobody, ultimately became a "god unto Pharaoh."[4]

The prince of Egypt met his Maker and his match on the back side of the desert at Mount Sinai, also known as Horeb (which means "dryness, heat, waste, solitude"). This protracted trial of faith would equip him to lead his church into that same barren wilderness and place of testing for another 40 years. Moses' submission to God's authority and his faithfulness to God's plan would one day bring him back to Horeb with a larger flock.

The divine intention is thus established—God begins His program with a man or woman, and then consummates that extended objective in and through a people, a family.

Ps. 106:23, KJV

Therefore He said that He would destroy them, had not Moses His chosen stood before Him in the breach [the gap in a broken wall], *to turn away His wrath, lest He should destroy them.*

John 1:17, KJV

For the law was given by [through] *Moses...*

Gal. 3:19, NAS

Why the Law then? It was added because of transgressions, having been ordained through angels by the agency of a mediator [go-between, arbitrator, middleman]...

Moses, the first son, was a mediator and reconciler. A peacemaker will consistently model God's chosen plan of reconciliation and forgiveness.

"Now the man Moses was very meek [exceedingly humble], above all the men which were upon the face of the earth" (Num. 12:3, KJV). His love for his nation was without peer. Jehovah was ready to disinherit this rebellious people and wipe them from the face of the earth. But Moses interceded, appealing to the honor of the Lord's name in the eyes of the nations, in spite of Jehovah's desire to make of him a new and greater nation!

Num. 14:17-20, KJV

And now, I beseech thee, let the power of my Lord be great, according as Thou hast spoken, saying,

> *The Lord is longsuffering, and of great mercy, forgiving iniquity and transgression, and by no means clearing the guilty, visiting the iniquity of the fathers upon the children unto the third and fourth generation.*
>
> *Pardon, I beseech thee, the iniquity of this people according unto the greatness of Thy mercy, and as Thou hast forgiven this people, from Egypt even until now.*
>
> *And the Lord said, I have pardoned according to thy word:*

Deut. 5:2,5, KJV

> *The Lord our God made a covenant with us in Horeb.*
>
> *(I stood between the Lord and you at that time, to show you the word of the Lord...).*[5]

God took Moses' humble and excellent "spirit" and put it on the 70 elders, multiplying the first son into a many-membered man.[6] Israel was blessed to have such godly leadership, especially when faced with the wrath of a foe like Seti or his successor Ramses.

The Persecution—God's Chosen Adversary

God's first son was a savior, mediator, reconciler, and intercessor. During the Exodus, Jehovah's chosen instrument encountered a fierce adversary. Pharaoh, the king and the god of Egypt, typifies satan, the "prince" and "god" of this world. This foundational principle, which runs throughout our story, must be clearly understood (see Jn. 12:31; 14:30; 16:11; Eph. 2:2 with 2 Cor. 4:4).

Egypt or Mizraim is the country in the northeast corner of Africa where the Israelites spent 430 years in servitude—it symbolizes the world and the bondage of sin.[7] The very word *Egypt* is from the Hebrew *Mitsrayim* (Strong's #4714); compare *matsowr* (Strong's #4692), which means, "a limit; something hemming in, (objectively) a mound (of besiegers), (abstractly) a siege, (figuratively) distress; or (subjectively) fastness." Its root *tsuwr* (Strong's #6696) means, "to cramp or confine."

The Pharaoh was probably the most important person in ancient Egyptian society. The Egyptians believed that he was a god, the very key to the nation's relationship to the cosmic gods of the universe. The ruling pharaoh was deemed to be the Son of Ra, the sun god, and the incarnation of their god Horus. Egyptians believed that Pharoah came from the gods with the divine responsibility to rule the land for them. Pharaoh's word to them was law, and, in their darkened minds, he owned everything.

Ex. 1:8-17, KJV

Now there arose up a new king over Egypt, which knew not Joseph.

And he said unto his people, Behold, the people of the children of Israel are more and mightier than we:

Come on, let us deal wisely with them; lest they multiply, and it come to pass, that, when there falleth out any war, they join also unto our enemies, and fight against us, and so get them up out of the land.

Therefore they did set over them taskmasters to afflict [oppress, depress] *them with their burdens. And they built for Pharaoh treasure cities, Pithom and Raamses.*

But the more they afflicted them, the more they multiplied and grew. And they were grieved because of the children of Israel.

And the Egyptians made the children of Israel to serve with rigour:

And they made their lives bitter with hard bondage, in mortar, and in brick, and in all manner of service in the field: all their service, wherein they made them serve, was with rigour.

And the king of Egypt spake to the Hebrew midwives, of which the name of the one was Shiphrah, and the name of the other Puah:

And he said, When ye do the office of a midwife to the Hebrew women, and see them upon the stools; if it be a son, then ye shall kill him: but if it be a daughter, then she shall live.

But the midwives feared God, and did not as the king of Egypt commanded them, but saved the men children alive.

The Living Bible for verse 11 says, "So the Egyptians made slaves of them and put brutal taskmasters over them to wear them down under heavy burdens while building the cities of Pithom and Rameses as supply centers for the king." The slave masters of Pharaoh made the people of God to serve with "rigour" or "harshness, severity, cruelty."

Gen. 3:15, KJV

And I will put enmity between thee [the serpent] *and the woman, and between thy seed and her seed; it* [He] *shall bruise thy head, and thou shalt bruise his heel.*

From the beginning, the spiritual battle between light and darkness has been over the seed. This "new king" who knew nothing of Joseph was Seti I, father to Ramses. In the New Testament, Stephen's speech to the Sanhedrin, recounting Israel's history, gives us a clearer picture of Seti's administration.

Acts 7:18-19, NIV

Then another king, who knew nothing about Joseph, became ruler of Egypt.

He dealt treacherously with our people and oppressed our forefathers by forcing them to throw out their newborn babies so that they would die.

Pharaoh hated Israel's seed and ordered the Hebrew midwives to kill every male baby. But Shiprah (whose name means "brightness, to glisten or make fair") and Puah ("splendid, brilliant") feared the Lord more than they feared this evil ruler. As a result,

God gave them "houses"—the Living Bible says that "He gave them children of their own" (Ex. 1:21).

Early on, when Pharaoh heard that Moses had killed the Egyptian, he sought to slay the hasty, would-be deliverer (Ex. 2:15). The young prince consequently fled into the land of Midian, where he remained for 40 years. There Moses providentially married Zipporah, daughter of Reuel (also called Jethro), and later received a revelation of Jehovah's name and his life's commission at the burning bush (Ex. 2:21; 3–4).

Seti died, and Israel "sighed by reason of [their] bondage" as Ramses came to the throne (Ex. 2:23). God saw their oppression and heard their groanings, and sent Moses back to the land of the Nile to bring His people up and out of the land of bondage.

Ex. 5:1-2, KJV

And afterward Moses and Aaron went in, and told Pharaoh, Thus saith the Lord God of Israel, Let My people go, that they may hold a feast unto Me in the wilderness.

And Pharaoh said, Who is the Lord, that I should obey His voice to let Israel go? I know not the Lord, neither will I let Israel go.

Moses' first encounter with Ramses was his demand to freely worship the living God. Let us be real clear here. The ultimate issue of the universe is worship. All conflict on the human plane centers in this issue of worship—whom will we worship and how will we worship? There is tremendous resistance to worship both outside and inside the Church. Outside political forces arrange themselves in an unholy alliance against the free worship of God. Inside the Church, religious tradition and manipulative leadership hinder the free access into the presence of God.

Pharaoh's response to Moses' request was the additional order and burden for the Israelites to gather their own straw for making bricks. Always the tactic of the devil and a beastly system is to "wear out [to mentally afflict or harass] the saints of the most High" (Dan. 7:25, KJV). The continual and constant pressures of financial hardship, troubling health, relational conflict, and job-related stress drain God's people of spiritual energy and deplete their emotional resources.

Ex. 6:1, KJV

Then the Lord said unto Moses, Now shalt thou see what I will do to Pharaoh: for with a strong hand shall he let them go, and with a strong hand shall he drive them out of his land.

Ex. 7:3, KJV

And I will harden Pharaoh's heart, and multiply My signs and My wonders in the land of Egypt.

2 Tim. 3:8-9, KJV

Now as Jannes and Jambres withstood Moses, so do these also resist the truth: men of corrupt minds, reprobate concerning the faith.

But they shall proceed no further: for their folly shall be manifest unto all men, as theirs also was.

God began to "harden" Ramses' heart.[8] This word means "dense, tough; to make stiff or stubborn." Pharaoh's magicians duplicated the miracle of Moses' rod by the power of satan, but their folly was soon swallowed up (Ex. 7:8-13). In the early days of Christianity, the evil sorcerers Simon and Barjesus were confronted and overcome by the apostolic ministries of Peter and Paul (Acts 8:9-11,18-24; 13:6-12).

All three scenarios prefigure a head-on, end-time, supernatural confrontation between the corporate son of hell and the corporate Son of God, the Church.

2 Cor. 2:11, NIV

in order that Satan might not outwit us. For we are not unaware of his schemes.

Moses' archenemy was cunningly deceitful. Ramses offered four compromises to the children of Israel. First, he summoned Moses and Aaron and said, "Go, sacrifice to your God here in the land" (Ex. 8:25, NIV).

Satan wants us to stay in his arena, and not to leave his territory. But his land is the world, and God hates a mixture in our worship. The ways of Egypt are the traditions of men. Moses replied, "That would not be right..." (Ex. 8:26, NIV).

Second, Pharaoh capitulated, "I will let you go to offer sacrifices to the Lord your God in the desert, but you must not go very far..." (Ex. 8:28, NIV).

The devil thinks, "Do not go so far that I cannot still get hold of you." The oppressor was willing to lengthen the chain, but it was still a chain! Real worship requires separation and complete liberty. Religious spirits sound like this: "Avoid extremes. Don't be a fanatic. Be sane. Be sensible. There is no need to cut loose from your old way of life, your old friends and associates."

Third, Moses returned to Ramses and declared, "We will go with our sons and daughters, flocks and herds...We will take everything with us; for we must all join in the holy pilgrimage." But Pharaoh would have none of that. He quickly retorted, "In the name of God I will not let you take your little ones!" (Ex. 10:9-10, TLB)

It is always the desire of the enemy to retain his dominion. If our children, our little ones, are still in Egypt, then we are still in Egypt! God must have all or nothing in our worship.

Fourth, Pharaoh ended his compromising ways with Moses with a final ploy. He called for Moses and said, "Go, worship the Lord. Even your women and children may go with you; only leave your flocks and herds behind" (Ex. 10:24, NIV).

God's first son refused. He knew that if the evil king could not keep them in or near the land, or prevent the whole family from worshiping, they would still need their flocks and herds, which constituted their ability to serve the Lord. This is what they owned, their property, their finance. Let us reply with Moses, the chosen of the Lord, "Therefore, our livestock too shall go with us; not a hoof shall be left behind..." (Ex. 10:26, NAS).

God severely judged the god and prince of Egypt. To deliver His people from Ramses' slavery and oppression, He sent astonishing signs and wonders to defeat Moses' adversary. These great judgments came in the form of ten plagues, recorded in Exodus chapters 7–12. Their purpose was to manifest the power of God, the "finger of God,"[9] to execute judgment against ten of the gods of Egypt, a picture of the present, transient cosmos (Num. 33:4):

1. The waters of the Nile were turned to blood—the world system is covered with death.

2. Frogs covered the land and entered the Egyptian homes—the world is filled with unclean spirits.

3. Lice were made to attack their persons—the world is filthy and unclean.

4. Swarms of flies invaded the nation—the world is full of the sons of Beelzebub, "the lord of the flies."

5. A grievous murrain or pestilence smote their cattle—the world is marked by the corrupt service of the natural man.

6. Boils and sores were sent to man and beast—the world is thus described in Isaiah 1:6.

7. Thunder and hail came upon Pharaoh's people—the world and its disobedient inhabitants abide under the wrath of God.

8. Locusts consumed all vegetation—the world is characterized by barren, desolate living.

9. Thick darkness overspread the land for three days—the world is alienated from Jesus Christ, the Light.

10. The firstborn of man and beast were slain—the world and its inhabitants are destined for the "second death" (Rev. 2:11).

Pharaoh had tried to kill the godly seed born to Amram and Jochebed. The god and prince of Egypt had been humbled and broken by the ten plagues at the mouth of Moses. The Red Sea would eventually swallow down Egypt's king and his army. The adversary of God's first son was soundly and completely defeated.

The Passover Principle—God's Chosen Season

Ex. 12:13, KJV

*And the blood shall be to you for a token upon the houses where ye are: and when I see the blood, I will **pass over** you, and the plague shall not be upon you to destroy you, when I smite the land of Egypt.*

Ex. 12:23, KJV

*For the Lord will pass through to smite the Egyptians; and when He seeth the blood upon the lintel, and on the two side posts, the Lord will **pass over** the door, and will not suffer the destroyer to come in unto your houses to smite you.*

The Passover principle flows throughout our story of God's three sons. Moses inaugurated the Passover. Jesus, the Word made flesh, was the prevailing Passover Lamb! The mature Church is about to pass over into the powers of the age to come.

Ex. 12:3, KJV

*Speak ye unto all the congregation of Israel, saying, In the tenth day of this month they shall take to them every man a lamb, according to the house of their fathers, a **lamb for an house**...*

The pattern was ordered and established in the days of Moses, the first son. When God got ready to bring a nation out of bondage, He put a lamb in every house! The following acrostic says it well:

Lay your life down at His feet,

And know at once His life complete.

More abundantly given, now abundantly shared,

Begotten of God, the Righteous Heir.

From the bosom of the Father,

Out of glory, there is no other

Royal Seed, for God has given

All He had, the Lamb of Heaven!

Hear this word, ye sons of men! See

On Calvary's tree, suspended high,

Unto you God's love draws nigh!

Sought by none, and yet He came that

Every man might know the Name of

                                                    ...Jesus.

Heb. 11:28, KJV

Through faith he [Moses] *kept the passover, and the sprinkling of blood, lest he that destroyed the firstborn should touch them.*

The Hebrew word for "Passover" is *Pecach* (Strong's #6453), and it means, "a pretermission, exemption; used only technically of the Jewish Passover (the festival or the victim)." It is derived from the verb *pacach* (Strong's #6452), which means, "to hop, (figuratively) spring or skip over (or spare); by implication, to hesitate; also (literally) to limp, to dance."

There are many Old Testament references to the Passover and the Feast of Unleavened Bread.[10] The Greek word, *Pascha*, is derived from the ancient Hebrew. Jehovah literally said to His people, "When I see the blood, I will dance over you!" That first Passover season was the night that God danced on the head of death!

Moses instituted and kept the Passover by faith. These instructions from the Lord were strangely new, unprecedented. The Passover was the first of the three great festivals given to the Hebrew people. It emphasized the sacrificial lamb offered without blemish in Egypt when the people of Israel were still slaves. The Hebrews smeared the blood of the lamb on their doorposts as a signal to God that He should "pass over" their houses when He destroyed all the firstborn of Egypt, including the firstborn in the palace of Ramses.

The Feast of Passover was observed on the 14th day of the first month, Abib, with the service beginning in the evening. It was on the evening of this day that Israel left Egypt. Passover commemorated this departure from Egypt in haste. Unleavened bread was used in the celebration because this showed that the people had no time to put leaven in their bread as they ate their final meal as slaves in Egypt. Passover was their last meal under Pharaoh's tyranny as they prepared for their journey of faith. It was followed by, and closely connected with, a seven days' festival of unleavened bread, to which the name Passover was also applied by extension.

At its first institution under Moses, just before the Exodus, the keeping of the Passover was as follows. Every head of a family chose a male lamb of the first year without blemish. This was done on the tenth day of Abib or Nisan, the first month of Israel's religious calendar. On the 14th, four days later, the animal was slain at twilight. According to the Karaite Jews, this took place between actual sunset and complete darkness. But the Pharisees and rabbis understood it as the time when the sun begins to descend to its real setting (from 3:00 to 6:00 p.m.).

The Passover ordinance included the following specific provisions (see Ex. 12:1-23):

1. Taking a lamb or kid without blemish for each household on the tenth of the month.

2. Killing the lamb on the 14th of Abib at evening.

3. Sprinkling the lamb's blood on doorposts and lintels of the houses in which it was to be eaten.

4. Roasting the whole lamb with fire, its head with its legs and innards—the lamb was not to be eaten raw nor sodden with water.

5. Eating unleavened bread and bitter herbs.

6. Eating the Passover meal in haste, with loins girded, shoes on the feet, and staff in hand.

7. Remaining in the house until the morning.

8. Burning all that remained—the Passover could be eaten only during the night.

More specifically, a bunch of hyssop was dipped in the blood of the animal and the blood was applied to the two posts and the lintel of the house where the meal was to be eaten. Then the whole animal, without a broken bone, was roasted and eaten by each family, including slaves and strangers, if they were circumcised. If the number of the family was too small, they might join a neighboring family. The lamb was eaten that same night with unleavened bread and bitter herbs, probably endives or wild lettuce. The rest of the meal was eaten the same evening, and all who partook had their loins girded, with shoes on their feet, and a staff in hand, ready to march out of Egypt. Whatever part of the lamb could not be eaten was to be burned the next morning; nothing of it was to be carried out of the house.

Moses, God's first son, kept God's word concerning the Passover by faith. Jehovah's instructions to his chosen instrument of deliverance seemed complete folly. Who had heard of such a thing? Yet Moses and his people strictly observed a plan that made no sense to the natural mind. It must be thus, for their keeping of this Feast was a matter of life and death!

Accordingly, Moses' obedience brought unprecedented blessings from the Lord. That night His church began a journey that was marked by the miraculous for another 40 years! Every wonder of

God's grace and favor upon Moses and his people happened for one simple reason—they had all eaten the Lamb!

Because of the prevailing Lamb from within, none were sick or feeble. Because of the Lamb from within, their bread and water did not diminish, and their shoes did not wear out. Every miracle that Israel experienced in their journey toward Canaan manifested from within them because of their corporate obedience—every miracle flowed forth from the indwelling Lamb!

The Provision—God's Chosen Transfer of Wealth (Health and Blessing)

Every 2,000 years, God has a "son." Moses, His chosen deliverer, introduces this pattern. Although he and his people suffered great persecution at the hands of Pharaoh, the blood of the first Passover lamb brought them out of bondage with great favor and blessing! Stephen's sermon to his elders, narrating Israel's history, calls this season of fulfillment "the time of the promise" (Acts 7:17).

Ex. 3:21-22, NIV

And I will make the Egyptians favorably disposed toward this people, so that when you leave you will not go empty-handed.

Every woman is to ask her neighbor and any woman living in her house for articles of silver and gold and for clothing, which you will put on your sons and daughters. And so you will plunder the Egyptians.

Ex. 12:35-36, TLB

And the people of Israel did as Moses said and asked the Egyptians for silver and gold jewelry and for clothing.

And the Lord gave the Israelis favor with the Egyptians, so that they gave them whatever they wanted. And the Egyptians were practically stripped of everything they owned!

Beginning with the first of His three sons, God arranged an unprecedented breakthrough of health and wealth upon His people. After all, what good is all that money if you are not alive to steward it? A nation was born overnight as the sons and daughters of Israel reaped over four hundred years of back wages. Jehovah had promised Abraham that the nation born out of his loins would come forth from their affliction with "great substance" (Gen. 15:14).

The word used here for "substance" means "property, riches, goods, or possessions." Dr. Luke, who wrote the Book of Acts, confirms that God "exalted" Israel with a "high arm" (signaling His power), raising them up to a place of opulence, dignity, and honor (Acts 13:17). The prophet Ezekiel passionately described God's blessings upon Moses' nation born in the land of the Nile.

Ezek. 16:8-13, KJV

Now when I passed by thee, and looked upon thee, behold, thy time was the time of love; and I spread My skirt over thee, and covered thy nakedness: yea, I sware unto thee, and entered into a covenant with thee, saith the Lord God, and thou becamest Mine.

Then washed I thee with water; yea, I throughly washed away thy blood from thee, and I anointed thee with oil.

I clothed thee also with broidered work, and shod thee with badgers' skin, and I girded thee about with fine linen, and I covered thee with silk.

I decked thee also with ornaments, and I put bracelets upon thy hands, and a chain on thy neck.

And I put a jewel on thy forehead, and earrings in thine ears, and a beautiful crown upon thine head.

Thus wast thou decked with gold and silver; and thy raiment was of fine linen, and silk, and broidered work; thou didst eat fine flour, and honey, and oil: and thou wast exceeding beautiful, and thou didst prosper into a kingdom.[11]

Moreover, the "I AM" God who commissioned His servant at the burning bush brought divine healing to Moses' congregation. As noted, there was a massive transfer of wealth during the times of God's first son. As an added blessing, those who left Egypt also experienced a supernatural demonstration of divine health!

Ps. 105:37, TLB

> *and brought His people safely out from Egypt, loaded with silver and gold; there were no sick and feeble folk among them then.*

Ex. 15:26, KJV

> *And said, If thou wilt diligently hearken to the voice of the Lord thy God, and wilt do that which is right in His sight, and wilt give ear to His commandments, and keep all His statutes, I will put none of these diseases upon thee, which I have brought upon the Egyptians: for I am the Lord that healeth thee.*

Ex. 23:25, KJV

> *And ye shall serve the Lord your God, and He shall bless thy bread, and thy water; and I will take sickness away from the midst of thee.*

The Hebrew word for "diseases" and "sickness" in these latter verses means "infirmity, sickness, weakness, affliction, or tiredness." The New American Standard Version for Exodus 23:25 declares that the Lord "will remove sickness from your midst." In the Book of Deuteronomy, the "second law" (where the key word is "remember"), Jehovah affirms this powerful aspect of covenant blessing!

Deut. 7:15, KJV

> *And the Lord will take away from thee all sickness, and will put none of the evil diseases of Egypt, which thou*

knowest, upon thee; but will lay them upon all them that hate thee.[12]

The church in the wilderness broke out of Egypt's bondage, anointed with heavenly health and wealth. These blessings followed them day by day throughout their journey. Consider these merciful miracles, signs, and wonders, which were new every morning!

1. A pillar of cloud shaded them by day (Ex. 13:21-22).

2. A pillar of fire warmed them by night (Ex. 13:21-22).

3. They ate manna from Heaven every morning (Ex. 16).

4. They drank water from the flinty rock every day (Ex. 17).

5. Their clothes and shoes did not wear out (Deut. 8:4; 29:5).

Jer 32:21, KJV

And hast brought forth Thy people Israel out of the land of Egypt with signs, and with wonders, and with a strong hand, and with a stretched out arm, and with great terror [an awe-inspiring object of reverence and fear].

All these blessings made this baby nation a thankful people. How sad it is that they later hardened their hearts through unbelief in the days of provocation (Num. 13–14; Heb. 3–4). But their beginnings were marked by gratitude and great generosity.

When Jehovah later instructed Moses to build the Tabernacle that He might dwell among His people, the young nation gave so much of their newly acquired assets that their leader had to tell them to stop!

As Bezaleel and Aholiab (the men appointed by God and given wisdom to build the Tabernacle) received this offering, they stood amazed as Israel "brought yet unto [them] free offerings every morning" (Ex. 36:3).

Ex. 36:4-7, NIV

So all the skilled craftsmen who were doing all the work on the sanctuary left their work and said to Moses, "The people are bringing more than enough for doing the work the Lord commanded to be done."

Then Moses gave an order and they sent this word throughout the camp: "No man or woman is to make anything else as an offering for the sanctuary." And so the people were restrained from bringing more,

because what they already had was more than enough to do all the work.

Ps. 105:24, KJV

And He increased His people greatly; and made them stronger than their enemies.

Much more could be said about Moses and his church. We have but introduced the model. Remember it. Every 2,000 years, God has a "son." That son is His chosen deliverer. That son faces tremendous pressure from God's chosen adversary. That son is raised up in God's chosen season of Passover. That son is released from bondage into an unlimited chosen provision of health, wealth, and blessing.

The first son, Moses, arbitrated the Law. The second son, the Pattern Son, is the Mediator of grace and truth. God was in Christ, reconciling the whole world back to Himself. This One faced down the pressures of the ages. This One *is* the prevailing Passover Lamb. This One rent the veil from the top to the bottom and dumped all of Heaven's resources upon a new humanity. This One is the Virgin Mary's baby boy. His is the greatest name of all.

Mt. 1:21, KJV

...and thou shalt call His name JESUS: for He shall save His people from their sins.

Chapter Three

The Second Son: The Master

Every 2,000 years, God has a "son." The first was Moses. The third is the Manchild, the mature Church. This chapter tells the story of the second Son—*the* Son—the Pattern Son. The Prophet like unto Moses is the antitype of the first son, and He is the prototype of the third. The model that began in the previous chapter now continues. What we learned about Moses and the first Passover is now set forth in the real Passover Lamb, humankind's only Savior.

Gal. 4:4-5, KJV

> *But when the fulness of the time was come, God sent forth His Son, made of a woman, made under the law,*
>
> *To redeem them that were under the law, that we might receive the adoption of sons.*

Moses and his helpers took nine months to bring the work of building the Old Testament Tabernacle to completion (Ex. 19:1; Num. 19:1-2).

Likewise, it took nine months for the Holy Spirit to form the body of Jesus, the true Tabernacle, in the womb of the Virgin Mary (Lk. 1:26-38; Heb. 10:5-10)!

The night of His Advent and birth was the first time that the angels had ever seen God. The Babe born in Bethlehem's manger was the image, the exact likeness, of the invisible, unseen God (Col. 1:15). As the heavens exploded with the thunderous praise of angels and the spirits of just men made perfect, the "I AM" who sent Moses down to Egypt wrapped Himself in flesh and came down here.

Mary then wrapped Him in swaddling clothes and laid Him in a manger, a feeding-trough, which was a crib or open box in a stable designed to hold fodder for feeding livestock. There He lay— eight pounds of love—all the fullness of the Godhead compressed into a tiny little body (Col. 1:19; 2:9)! The eternal Word (*Logos*), the sum total of everything that God would ever say to humankind, had just become flesh.[1]

My book *The Time of the Messiah* (Shippensburg, PA: Destiny Image, 1996, pp. 17-18) powerfully narrates the season of His incarnation. These words open its Preface:

"Judea, 4 B.C., 20 centuries ago…

"Sanctified hope is whispering like a still, small voice in the hearts of devout Jews throughout the land. No clear prophetic voice has been heard for 400 years, yet the spirit of prophecy is fluttering afresh over the ancient writings of Isaiah and Micah like a great bird anticipating its descent.

"Religious systems and would-be prophets are settled in their convictions as to the purpose and manner of Messiah's advent.

"The injustice of worldly Roman oppression is crying out for vengeance. Poverty, ignorance, and disease continue to plunder the people.

"Inquiring angels are assembling for choir practice.

"Demons are snickering, ignorant and unchallenged.

"Wicked King Herod is proud of his 'politically correct' rebuilt temple.

"The priestly house of Zacharias and Elizabeth is quiet.

"A young couple from the house of David are laughing as they plan their wedding and their future together.

"Somewhere in Jerusalem, an old man is still alive because God's unfulfilled promise is stronger than the last enemy.

"In a small prayer chamber inside the house of the Lord, an old woman weeps and prays, as she has done for the past 80 years.

"Gabriel is reminding Daniel of his famous prophecy.

"Faithful shepherds, like David, are singing over their folds.

"Wise men are scanning the heavens.

"The heart of the sovereign God is stirring with the awareness of an everlasting, intertheistic covenant. The bosom of the Father is swelling with love, inspired to speak His Word.

"The Holy Spirit, the power of the Highest, stands ready to overshadow a habitation of purity.

"The stage is set. It's time for the Deliverer to appear."

The Person—God's Chosen Deliverer

God's first son delivered one embryonic nation from the tyranny of a mere Egyptian Pharaoh. Jesus saved all of creation from the bondage of sin and satan. Moses had been extracted from the muddy waters of the Nile. Mankind's only Savior was drawn from the dark, unlit waters of a virgin womb that had never known a man. Jehovah handpicked his servant Moses by a burning bush. Earth's Messiah, the true Vine, was the Servant of Jehovah, the "elect" or "chosen" of God.[2]

Before time had begun or anything had been created, there was a meeting in the invisible realm. The Father was there. The Son was there. And the Holy Ghost was there, taking the "minutes" of the meeting, which would later become "the volume of the book" (Ps. 40:7; Heb. 10:7).

The Father said to the Son, "Thou art My Son; this day have I begotten Thee. Ask of Me, and I shall give Thee the heathen [the nations] for Thine inheritance, and the uttermost parts of the earth for Thy possession...Thou art a priest for ever after the order of Melchizedek" (Ps. 2:7-8; 110:4).

The Son replied, "Lo, I come (in the volume of the book it is written of Me,) to do Thy will, O God" (Heb. 10:7).

Our King is the color purple, that mysterious mingling of the blue of Heaven and the red clay of earth. Jesus is very God and very man, the God-man who came to do the will of His Father.

Heb. 2:17, KJV

Wherefore in all things it behoved Him to be made like unto His brethren, that He might be a merciful and faithful high priest in things pertaining to God, to make reconciliation for the sins of the people.

Job 9:33, KJV

Neither is there any daysman betwixt us, that might lay his hand upon us both [God and man].

The New International Version of this latter verse says, "If only there were someone to arbitrate between us." The Living Bible adds, "there is no umpire between us, no middle man, no mediator to bring us together." Jesus, the second Son, the Pattern Son, brought reconciliation by arbitration. God and man had reached an impasse— sin, and the penalty of sin, which is death. Fully representing both sides, divine and human, Jesus' word became *the* Word, having swallowed up the previous Law of Moses (see Mt. 5–7).

Ps. 115:16, NIV

The highest heavens belong to the Lord, but the earth He has given to man.

Ezek. 22:30, KJV

And I sought for a man among them, that should make up the hedge, and stand in the gap before Me for the land, that I should not destroy it: but I found none.

Ezekiel chapter 22 describes the land of Judah in crisis and chaos. Sin had contaminated an entire society, polluting the prophets, the priests, the princes (kings), and the people. God searched in vain for a "man" to do His will. Whatever God does in the earth, He is bound by His word to do it through a man. When Jesus, the fleshly answer to Job's ancient cry, came to redeem us, He could not do it as God. He had to do it as a *man*! Though He was God in the flesh, Heaven's Lamb had to be tempted in all points like as we are, yet without sin.[3]

The rod of Moses became the rod of God (Ex. 4). The second Son was "the rod out of the stem [David] of Jesse," and the Head of the many-membered Man "whose name is The Branch" (Is. 11:1; Zech. 6:12).

Moses became a god unto Pharaoh (Ex. 7:1). Jesus *is* Elohim, the Creator. He *is* God!

As did Moses, the second Son went into the wilderness in behalf of His people (Lk. 4:1-14). As with Moses, Jesus' submission to divine order and authority, and His faithfulness to His Father's plan brought Him to the mountains of transfiguration, crucifixion, and ascension to become the embodiment of the Law.

Eph. 2:14-16, TLB

For Christ Himself is our way of peace. He has made peace between us Jews and you Gentiles by making us all one family, breaking down the wall of contempt that used to separate us.

By His death He ended the angry resentment between us, caused by the Jewish laws that favored the Jews and excluded the Gentiles, for He died to annul that whole system of Jewish laws. Then He took the two groups that had been opposed to each other and made them parts of Himself; thus He fused us together to become one new person, and at last there was peace.

As parts of the same body, our anger against each other has disappeared, for both of us have been reconciled to God. And so the feud ended at last at the cross.

Col. 1:20, KJV

And, having made peace through the blood of His cross, by Him to reconcile all things unto Himself; by Him, I say, whether they be things in earth, or things in heaven.

Patterned after His predecessor Moses, Jesus is the consummate Mediator and Reconciler, the One who came to redeem and forgive.

"He is our peace" (Eph. 2:14, KJV). The second Son is the "Prince of Peace" (Is. 9:6), the benefactor and recipient of peace; and He is the "King of peace" (Heb. 7:2), the administrator of peace. Jesus, the full-grown Son, is the supreme Peacemaker (Mt. 5:9).

In the Old Covenant, God took the "spirit" of Moses and put it on the 70 elders; in the New Testament, the Father sent the Spirit of His Son into our hearts, whereby we worship, "Abba, Father."[4]

Moses was the "head" of the Old Testament nation, the church in the wilderness. Jesus Christ is the Head of the New Testament holy nation comprised of Jew and Greek. His Church is the Nation from among the nations, the one new breed from among the races. A people who were not a people have now become *the* people of God (1 Pet. 2:9-10). The six chapters of Paul's letter to the Ephesians set forth Jesus to be the Head of the Church, the Temple, the Family, the Body, the Woman, and the Army, respectively.

As was Moses, Jesus Christ was sent as a chosen Deliverer. Baby Moses faced the wrath of Seti, Pharaoh of Egypt. Likewise, the jealous rage and diabolical butchery of Herod the Great threatened the second Son, the newly born Pattern Son, and the Seed of God.

The Persecution—God's Chosen Adversary

Mt. 2:13-21, KJV

And when they were departed, behold, the angel of the Lord appeareth to Joseph in a dream, saying, Arise, and take the young child and his mother, and flee into Egypt, and be thou there until I bring thee word: for Herod will seek the young child to destroy him.

When he arose, he took the young child and his mother by night, and departed into Egypt:

And was there until the death of Herod: that it might be fulfilled which was spoken of the Lord by the prophet, saying, Out of Egypt have I called My son.

Then Herod, when he saw that he was mocked of the wise men, was exceeding wroth, and sent forth, and slew all the children that were in Bethlehem, and in all the coasts thereof, from two years old and under, according to the time which he had diligently inquired of the wise men.

Then was fulfilled that which was spoken by Jeremy the prophet, saying,

In Rama was there a voice heard, lamentation, and weeping, and great mourning, Rachel weeping for her children, and would not be comforted, because they are not.

But when Herod was dead, behold, an angel of the Lord appeareth in a dream to Joseph in Egypt,

Saying, Arise, and take the young child and his mother, and go into the land of Israel: for they are dead which sought the young child's life.

And he arose, and took the young child and his mother, and came into the land of Israel.

The word *Herod*, a compound of the Greek word *heros* and transliterated to mean "a hero; heroic," is the surname of a royal family. These Jewish kings flourished in the times of Christ and the early apostles. Among them were Herod the Great (son of the Idumean Roman procurator, Antipater); Herod Antipas (tetrarch over Galilee who beheaded John the Baptist and who later tried Jesus); Herod Agrippa I (who killed James and imprisoned Peter); and Herod Agrippa II (who was almost persuaded by the preaching of Paul). Moses' nemesis was Ramses. Baby Jesus' chosen adversary was the first of the aforementioned Herods, Herod the Great.

Herod the Great (so named as the eldest son of Antipater of Idumaea) was appointed king of Judaea in 40 B.C. by the Roman Senate, and took possession of his kingdom three years later. The Idumaens were of Edomite stock, descendants of Esau.[5]

Herod was a ruthless fighter, a cunning negotiator, and a subtle diplomat. The Romans appreciated the way he subdued opposition and maintained order among the Jewish people. The son of Antipater was brave and skilled in war, learned and sagacious, but also extremely suspicious and cruel. He was a heathen in practice and a monster in character.

Herod put to death many of the Jews who opposed his government. The first act of his reign was to exterminate the entire royal family of the Hasmoneans. His own wife Mariamne, of the Hasmonaean line, also became a victim of his suspicion and brutality, along with his mother-in-law Alexandra, and even his two sons (Alexander and Aristobulus) that Mariamne had borne to him. At last, on his own deathbed, just five days before he breathed his last, this evil ruler ordered his son Antipater to be slain. It is no wonder that Caesar Augustus should have ridiculed this Jewish king, saying, "It is better to be Herod's hog than to be his son!"

Herod's acts of bloodshed, his love and imitation of Roman customs and institutions, and the burdensome taxes imposed upon his subjects so alienated the Jews that he was unable to regain their favor by his splendid restoration of the temple[6] and other acts of munificence.

This immoral and depraved king was finally the victim of an incurable and loathsome disease. He became more irritable as the malady progressed, and he made both himself and his court unutterably miserable. The Jewish historian Josephus writes this epitaph: "A man he was of great barbarity toward all men equally, and a slave to his passions; but above the consideration of what was right..." (Ant, XVII, viii, 1). The incarnation of brute lust, Herod the Great died unmourned and unbeloved by his own people, to pass into history as a name soiled by violence and blood.

Gen. 3:15, KJV

And I will put enmity [hatred, hostility] *between thee and the woman, and between thy seed and her seed; it shall bruise thy head, and thou shalt bruise his heel.*

Gen. 3:15, TLB

From now on you and the woman will be enemies, as will your offspring and hers. You will strike his heel, but he will crush your head.

Herod the Great died at 70 years of age, in the 37th year of his reign. In his closing years, John the Baptist and Jesus Christ were born. To assure his continued rule, this maniac slaughtered all male infants who could possibly be considered legal heirs to the throne. The Gospel of Matthew narrates that this evil monarch commanded that all the male children less than two years old in Bethlehem were to be slain. This demonized man, a willing pawn in the hand of his father the devil, hated the royal Messianic Seed.

Mt 2:7-12, NIV

Then Herod called the Magi secretly and found out from them the exact time the star had appeared.

He sent them to Bethlehem and said, "Go and make a careful search for the child. As soon as you find Him, report to me, so that I too may go and worship Him."

After they had heard the king, they went on their way, and the star they had seen in the east went ahead of them until it stopped over the place where the child was.

When they saw the star, they were overjoyed.

On coming to the house, they saw the child with His mother Mary, and they bowed down and worshiped him. Then they opened their treasures and presented Him with gifts of gold and of incense and of myrrh.

And having been warned in a dream not to go back to Herod, they returned to their country by another route.

My book *The Time of the Messiah* (Shippensburg, PA: Destiny Image, 1996, pp. 19-20) reveals that Jesus' coming to this earth was:

1. A time of *wonder* (Mt. 1:18-25).

   The Messiah cannot be explained!

2. A time of *witness* (Lk. 1:1-80).

   The Messiah cannot be silenced!

3. A time of *warfare* (Mt. 2:13-23; Lk. 2:1-52).

   The Messiah cannot be contaminated!

4. A time of *worship* (Mt. 2:1-12).

   The Messiah cannot be dethroned!

A virgin womb, faithful shepherds, a sure prophetic witness from both Prophet Simeon and Prophetess Anna, accompanied by wisdom from above (Jesus at the age of 12) had kept the Seed pure (Lk. 2:1-52). But Messiah's time of *warfare* is especially emphasized in the horrible attempt of Herod the Great to kill the baby Messiah, the anointed Seed, and the rightful King of the Jews. The narrative of Messianic warfare set forth in Matthew 2:13-23 reveals the pattern of casting down thrones.[7]

This principle was illustrated in the last chapter by Pharaoh's extermination of the Hebrew babies in the time of Moses. It will be demonstrated again in the next chapter as the great red dragon stands before the sun-clothed woman of Revelation 12, to devour her manchild as soon as he is born. Two other scriptural examples of this overthrowing of kings is the downfall of King Saul and the coronation of King David, and wicked Queen Athaliah's unthinkable effort to kill her own grandchildren, including little King Joash of Judah (2 Chron. 22–23).

Herod the Great, like Pharaoh, pictures an angry devil, "king over all the children of pride" (Job 41:34), who comes to the earth with great wrath. He recognizes that he has but a "short [slight] time" (Rev. 12:12). Herod also represents the carnal mind, the arrogant king of self.[8] All great men of the flesh are disqualified in the day when God reveals His Son. The Almighty is not interested in what Herod thinks or says.

Simply put, Herod represents anyone or anything that tries to stand in the way of the "holy thing" (Lk. 1:35), that which purposes to destroy or usurp the rightful reign of the divine Seed in order to preserve a lesser authority. Thus, Herod characterizes the spirit of "antichrist" (1 Jn. 2:18-22; 4:3; 2 Jn. 1:7).

The Herods were of Idumean blood, descendants of Esau, the man of the flesh. Their family spirit is like unto Ishmael, who persecuted Isaac (Gen. 21:9-10; Gal. 4:28-31). As the son of promise intimidated the wild son of Hagar, so King Jesus was a threat to Herod's throne.

Mt. 2:13-15, NIV

When they had gone, an angel of the Lord appeared to Joseph in a dream. "Get up," he said, "take the child and his mother and escape to Egypt. Stay there until I tell you, for Herod is going to search for the child to kill Him."

So he got up, took the child and His mother during the night and left for Egypt,

where he stayed until the death of Herod. And so was fulfilled what the Lord had said through the prophet: "Out of Egypt I called My son."

Joseph's and Mary's flight into Egypt held a threefold strategy:

1. To protect the divine Child, the Pattern Son, from His enemies.

2. To show the divine care and valuation of the holy Child.

3. To make His childhood sufferings the antitype to the story of Moses' preservation from the wrath of Pharaoh.

The angel warned Joseph that Herod was plotting against Messiah to utterly destroy Him. Joseph obeyed at once, taking his family to Egypt, fulfilling the words of the prophet Hosea.[9] All three of God's "sons" have been called out of Egypt's bondage, out of the world system, and everything in it.[10]

Mt. 2:16, NIV

When Herod realized that he had been outwitted by the Magi, he was furious, and he gave orders to kill all the boys in Bethlehem and its vicinity who were two years old and under, in accordance with the time he had learned from the Magi.

Mt. 2:16, TLB

Herod was furious when he learned that the astrologers had disobeyed him. Sending soldiers to Bethlehem, he ordered them to kill every baby boy two years old and under, both in the town and on the nearby farms, for the astrologers had told him the star first appeared to them two years before.

Wise men still outsmart foolish rulers. The King James Version of this verse says that Herod "sent forth" wicked men to murder the promised Seed. This is the word *apostello*, and it reveals that the days of God's sons are marked by the appearance and devilish activity of "false apostles" (2 Cor. 11:3; Rev. 2:2). The senseless killing of babies shamelessly marks these times—abortion is America's national evil.

Mt. 2:17-23, NIV

Then what was said through the prophet Jeremiah was fulfilled:

"A voice is heard in Ramah, weeping and great mourning, Rachel weeping for her children and refusing to be comforted, because they are no more."

After Herod died, an angel of the Lord appeared in a dream to Joseph in Egypt

and said, "Get up, take the child and His mother and go to the land of Israel, for those who were trying to take the child's life are dead."

So he got up, took the child and His mother and went to the land of Israel.

But when he heard that Archelaus was reigning in Judea in place of his father Herod, he was afraid to go there. Having been warned in a dream, he withdrew to the district of Galilee,

and he went and lived in a town called Nazareth. So was fulfilled what was said through the prophets: "He will be called a Nazarene."

Herod the Great, the archenemy of God's second Son, finally breathed out his last foul breath. Joseph brought his family back from Egypt and settled in the city of Nazareth.

Go ahead, Joseph, get out your tools and build a playground in your backyard for the Seed. You won't have to run from town to town anymore. There is nothing now to fear. Herod is dead! The Messiah is safe! Put down roots in Galilee and, for the first time in a long time, just rest as you enjoy watching the Seed grow into manhood.

Is. 26:13-14, NIV

O Lord, our God, other lords besides You have ruled over us, but Your name alone do we honor.

They are now dead, they live no more; those departed spirits do not rise. You punished them and brought them to ruin; You wiped out all memory of them.

Ps. 30:5, KJV

...weeping may endure for a night, but joy cometh in the morning.

The Passover Principle—God's Chosen Season

Ex. 12:13, KJV

And the blood shall be to you for a token upon the houses where ye are: and when I see the blood, I will pass over you, and the plague shall not be upon you to destroy you, when I smite the land of Egypt.

Heb. 11:28, KJV

Through faith he [Moses] *kept the passover...*

Every 2,000 years, God has a "son." The first was Moses, delivered from the power of Pharaoh by the blood of a Passover lamb. Both Testaments repeatedly affirm the truth that the Lord Jesus Christ, the second Son, *is* the prevailing Lamb!

Is. 53:7, KJV

He was oppressed, and He was afflicted, yet He opened not His mouth: He is brought as a lamb to the slaughter, and as a sheep before her shearers is dumb, so He openeth not His mouth.

Jn. 1:29, KJV

The next day John seeth Jesus coming unto him, and saith, Behold the Lamb of God, which taketh away the sin of the world.

Acts 8:32, KJV

The place of the scripture which He read was this, He was led as a sheep to the slaughter; and like a lamb dumb before His shearer, so opened He not His mouth:

1 Cor. 5:7, KJV

...For even Christ our passover is sacrificed for us.

1 Pet. 1:19, KJV

But with the precious blood of Christ, as of a lamb without blemish and without spot:

The Greek word for "lamb" in these New Testament passages is *amnos*. The definite article is used in John's Gospel, pointing Him out as the expected One, the personal fulfillment and embodiment of all that had been indicated in the Old Testament. He alone is the One by whose sacrifice our deliverance from divine judgment was to be obtained. In Acts and First Peter, the absence of the article stresses the nature and character of His sacrifice as set forth in the symbolism.

The slain Lamb is unveiled as the centerpiece of the Book of Revelation. Throughout the Apocalypse, the word *Lamb* is mentioned exactly 27 times (the number of books in our New Testament)! This is *arnion* (Strong's #721), a different word from amnos, and it means, "a lambkin."

Arnion is a diminutive of *aren*, which means, "a lamb (as a male)." It in turn is taken from *arsen* ("a male or man, as stronger for lifting"); and from *airo* ("to lift up, to take up or away, to remove; figuratively, to expiate sin").

Jesus Christ, the Lamb of God, was lifted up on Calvary to take away our sin! The Book of Revelation is the unveiling of Jesus Christ as the slain Lamb. John the Revelator saw the Lamb to be the Lion, and the Lion to be the Lamb!

Rev. 5:12, KJV

Worthy is the Lamb that was slain...

Rev. 13:8, KJV

...the book of life of the Lamb slain from the foundation of the world.

Rev. 17:14, KJV

These shall make war with the Lamb, and the Lamb shall overcome them: for He is Lord of lords, and King of kings: and they that are with Him are called, and chosen, and faithful.

Rev. 19:7,9, KJV

Let us be glad and rejoice, and give honour to Him: for the marriage of the Lamb is come, and His wife hath made herself ready.

Blessed are they which are called unto the marriage supper of the Lamb...

Rev. 22:1, KJV

And he showed me a pure river of water of life, clear as crystal, proceeding out of the throne of God and of the Lamb.

As noted in the previous chapter, the Passover ordinance included the following eight specific provisions (Ex. 12:1-23):

First, the people selected a lamb, a kid without blemish, for each household on the tenth of the month. Jesus Christ was the Lamb slain from the foundation of the world. He was Jehovah's elect, the chosen One, taken from the bosom of the Father and given to the world.[11]

Second, they killed the lamb on the 14th of Abib at evening. It had to be inspected for four days to insure its purity. One day is with the Lord as one thousand years. From Adam to Jesus is four "days." Jesus, the spotless, sinless Son of God, waited patiently for four "days" from the time of the first Adam to be killed on the evening of the 14th of Abib (which means "to be tender; green, as an ear of grain").[12] Fourteen is the biblical number denoting Passover, salvation, and sacrifice.

Third, the people dipped a bunch of hyssop in blood and then sprinkled the entrance doorposts and lintels of the houses where the lamb was to be eaten. The blood of Jesus has been applied to the doorway of our hearts.[13] This double cross on the Israelites' doors pointed to Calvary's bloody hill and to Him who is the only Door to God (Jn. 10:1-9). Interestingly, no blood was to be sprinkled on the threshold, to teach a reverent regard for the blood of Christ. Men should not tread underfoot the Son of God, nor count the blood of the covenant wherewith they were sanctified an unholy thing (Heb 10:29).

Fourth, the people roasted the whole animal, without a broken bone, with fire. The lamb was not to be eaten raw nor sodden with water. It was completely consumed (including the head as well as legs and innards). One lamb was eaten by each family, including slaves and strangers, if they were circumcised. If the number of the family was too small, they might join a neighboring family. We must never "water down" the preaching of the cross! The fire of God's zeal took Jesus to Calvary, where not one bone was broken. We must consume the Lamb, appropriating His mind, His walk, and His inmost affections. Though everyone must know the Lamb personally—a Lamb for a house—Jesus died to join together every family of the earth.[14]

Fifth, they ate the Passover lamb with unleavened bread and bitter herbs. Unleavened bread is squeezed or compressed bread, made heavy without leaven, or yeast. The Lord Jesus Christ is the Bread from heaven. His life is without sin and corruption, free of all malice and wickedness. In the Garden of "Gethsemane," which means "olive press," Jesus took the cup overflowing with the bitter bondage of humanity's sin, and on the cross He drank it all down.[15]

Sixth, the people ate the Paschal meal in haste, with their loins girded, and shoes on the feet, and staff in hand, ready to leave Egypt. Jesus, the second Son, the Pattern Son, is girded about with priestly garments, unlimited power, majesty and strength, righteousness and faithfulness, wrought gold (the divine nature), and the servant's towel. The Passover Lamb is King of kings, wearing shoes of dominion and sonship, and carrying about the staff, the rod or the scepter of His Kingdom.[16]

Seventh, the people remained in the house until the morning, staying obediently under the covenantal protection of the blood. The Pattern Son is the perfect Son. He delighted to do the will of His Father, and always did those things that pleased Him. Jesus learned obedience by the things that He suffered, ever staying within the bounds of the predetermined, everlasting covenant.[17]

Finally, they burned all of the Passover lamb that remained, for it could only be eaten during the night. None was to remain until the morning (dawn, daybreak). Whatever part of the lamb that could not be eaten was burned the next morning; nothing of it was to be carried out of the house. This was done primarily to prevent putrefaction. A thing offered to God should not be subjected to corruption, which in such hot countries it must speedily undergo. Thus the body of our blessed Lord, the Paschal Lamb offered as our sacrifice, saw no corruption.[18]

As noted, Moses kept the first Passover by faith. Even so the offering of Jesus Christ, the Father's chosen instrument of deliverance, seemed unthinkable. Such a plan is absurdity and foolishness to the natural mind. It has to be, for it remains a matter of life and death!

1 Cor. 1:18-19, NIV

For the message of the cross is foolishness to those who are perishing, but to us who are being saved it is the power of God.

For it is written: "I will destroy the wisdom of the wise; the intelligence of the intelligent I will frustrate."

1 Cor. 1:18-19, TLB

I know very well how foolish it sounds to those who are lost, when they hear that Jesus died to save them. But we who are saved recognize this message as the very power of God.

For God says, "I will destroy all human plans of salvation no matter how wise they seem to be, and ignore the best ideas of men, even the most brilliant of them."

I Jn. 5:12, KJV

He that hath the Son hath life; and he that hath not the Son of God hath not life.

The Provision—God's Chosen Transfer of Wealth (Health and Blessing)

Every 2,000 years, God has a "son." Moses, the hero of the Exodus, launched this pattern. Although he and his people suffered great persecution at the hands of Pharaoh, the blood of the first Passover lamb brought them out of bondage with great favor and blessing!

When the Old Testament church in the wilderness came out of Egypt, their pockets were filled and overflowing with 430 years of back wages. Jehovah abundantly blessed Moses' new congregation, bringing Israel "out of the land of Egypt with signs, and with wonders, and with a strong hand, and with a stretched out arm, and with great terror [as an awe-inspiring object of fear and reverence]" (Jer. 32:21, KJV). Moreover, He kept them free of all disease (Ex. 15:26), for "there were no sick and feeble folk among them" (Ps. 105:37, TLB).

Lk. 9:28-31, KJV

And it came to pass about an eight days after these sayings, He took Peter and John and James, and went up into a mountain to pray.

And as He prayed, the fashion of His countenance was altered, and His raiment was white and glistering.

And, behold, there talked with Him two men, which were Moses and Elias:

*Who appeared in glory, and spake of His **decease** which He should accomplish at Jerusalem.*

It is awesome to consider that the first son showed up on the Mount of Transfiguration to converse with the second Son! Moses came with Elijah to talk with Jesus about His "decease." Several other translations render this as His "departure." This is the Greek word *exodos* (Strong's #1841), and it means, "an exit; (figuratively) death." Thayer's Lexicon adds, "the close of one's career, one's final fate; departure from life." *Exodos* (English, "exodus") is taken from *ek* ("out of") and *hodos* ("way, road, path"). It is used by Paul in Hebrews 11:22 to reference the "departing" of Israel from Egypt, and by Peter in Second Peter 1:15 with regard to his "decease" or death.

Moses came to comfort Jesus concerning His "exodus," which would be accomplished in His "decease" at Jerusalem on Golgotha's hill! Jesus' "departure" happened on an old rugged cross, where He embarrassed principalities and powers, and led captive a host of captives (Ps. 68:18; Eph. 4:8; Col. 2:15).

Mt. 27:50-53, KJV

Jesus, when He had cried again with a loud voice, yielded up the ghost.

And, behold, the veil of the temple was rent in twain from the top to the bottom; and the earth did quake, and the rocks rent;

And the graves were opened; and many bodies of the saints which slept arose,

And came out of the graves after His resurrection, and went into the holy city, and appeared unto many.

When Moses led his church out of Egypt, the Red Sea and the Jordan parted before them. When the Pattern Son led captivity captive, bringing out His Church and all creation with Him, the veil was rent from the top to the bottom![19]

The first son's "church" came out with unprecedented health and wealth. Jesus' rending of the veil loosed "all spiritual blessings in heavenly places in Christ Jesus" (Eph. 1:3)! Moses and his people got a taste of heaven with the daily manna that fell. The King of glory loosed *all* of Heaven upon us through the Person of the Holy Spirit, His Spirit!

He who is the Tree of life was stretched out on the tree of death. On Mount Calvary, suspended between Heaven and earth, the Pattern Son, humankind's only Savior, completely fulfilled the anointed words of the prophet Isaiah, "And on this mountain He will swallow up the covering which is over all peoples, even the veil which is stretched over all nations. He will swallow up death for all time, and the Lord God will wipe tears away from all faces, and He will remove the reproach of His people from all the earth; for the Lord has spoken" (Is. 25:7-8, NAS).

Jesus' finished work—His death, burial, resurrection, ascension, and coronation—declared Him to be "the Son of God with power" (Rom. 1:4). Jesus is now "the heir of all things" in Heaven, in earth, and under the earth (Heb. 1:2).

Rom. 15:8, KJV

Now I say that Jesus Christ was a minister of the circumcision for the truth of God, to confirm [secure] *the promises made unto the fathers.*

The God of Abraham, Isaac, and Jacob became the God of Moses, the first son. The second Son, the greatest Son, the Heir[20] of all things, "confirmed" or "made firm, established, made sure" every promise that God made to the "fathers." Who were these fathers? Doctor Luke, who wrote the Book of Acts, tells us.

Acts 3:13, KJV

The God of Abraham, and of Isaac, and of Jacob, the God of our fathers, hath glorified His Son Jesus...

The fathers were Abraham, Isaac, and Jacob. Jesus, the Pattern Son, is the Heir and Benefactor of every covenant. He secured every promise that God made to these three great patriarchs, Abraham, Isaac, and Jacob, as revealed throughout the Book of Genesis.[21] How marvelous then to consider that we His children or sons are "heirs; heirs of God, and joint-heirs with Christ" (Rom. 8:17)!

Mt 28:18-20, NIV

Then Jesus came to them and said, "All authority in heaven and on earth has been given to Me.

Therefore go and make disciples of all nations, baptizing them in the name of the Father and of the Son and of the Holy Spirit,

and teaching them to obey everything I have commanded you. And surely I am with you always, to the very end of the age."

The word for "authority" ("power" in the King James Version) in Matthew 28:18 is *exousia*, (Strong's #1849), and it means, "(in the sense of ability); privilege, force, capacity, competency, freedom, or mastery; delegated influence." It is rendered in the King James Version as "authority, jurisdiction, liberty, power, right, strength."

Thayer's Lexicon adds that *exousia* means, "power of choice, liberty of doing as one pleases, permission; the power of authority (influence) and of right (privilege); the power of rule or government (the power of him whose will and commands must be submitted to by others and obeyed)." Universally, *exousia* is "authority over mankind; metonymically, it is the sign of regal authority, a crown." Vine's Dictionary notes that *exousia* denotes "authority" (from the impersonal verb *exesti*, "it is lawful").

The rod of Moses became the rod of God. Jesus, the second Son, *is* the Rod of God! The scepter (baton of royalty) of His Kingdom is a scepter of righteousness (Heb. 1:8). All executive privilege and governmental authority centers in His glorious Person—*in* Heaven and *on* earth! His Word is law—He is the Word! He embodies the Law! His all-authority is the very basis and foundation of the Great Commission.

Ps. 24:1, KJV

> *The earth is the Lord's, and the fulness thereof; the world, and they that dwell therein.*

Ps. 24:1, TLB

> *The earth belongs to God! Everything in all the world is His!*

The earth does not belong to the devil and his crowd. Satan may be the god of this world (the transient cosmos), but he is not the god of our world! The earth belongs to our Lord and His Church, Mr. and Mrs. Jesus Christ, "heirs together of the grace of life" (1 Pet. 3:7).

The Lord Jesus Christ subdued "all things" unto Himself, and has bequeathed to us "all things" that pertain unto life and godliness (Phil. 3:21; 2 Pet. 1:3).[22] Moses and his congregation came out of Egypt with great blessing, a massive transfer of health and wealth. Jesus and His holy flock made their "exodus" at Calvary. His finished work rent the veil, releasing everything that had been hidden for ages and generations.

Phil. 4:13,19, KJV

> *I can do all things through Christ which strengtheneth me.*

> *But my God shall supply all your need according to His riches in glory by Christ Jesus.*

To catch but a glimpse of the abundance of these "riches" in Christ Jesus, consider the various names for God in the Old Testament. God's name unfolds all that He *is*, all that He *has*, and all that He *does*. The name of the Lord Jesus Christ, the Name above every name,[23] embodies each and all of these covenantal blessings, which unfold in the various *El* and *Jehovah* names for God:

The El names:[24]

1. *El*, the strong and mighty One—His power and strength.

2. *Elohim*, the Creator God—His creativity and ingenuity.

3. *El-Shaddai*, the breasted One—His compassion and intimacy.

4. *El-Elyon*, the Most High God, Possessor of Heaven and earth—His dominion.

The *Jehovah* compound names:[25]

1. *Jireh*, the Lord who sees and provides—His provision.

2. *Rapha*, the Lord who heals—His healing (spirit, soul, and body).

3. *Nissi*, the Lord our Banner—His victory.

4. *M'Kaddesh*, the Lord who sanctifies—His holiness.

5. *Shalom*, the Lord our Peace—His peace.

6. *Shaphat*, the Lord our Judge—His judgment.

7. *Rohi*, the Lord our Shepherd—His pastoral care.

8. *Hosenu*, the Lord our Maker—His power to change things.

9. *Tsidkenu*, the Lord our Righteousness—His righteousness.

10. *Shammah*, the Lord is there—His faithfulness and glory.

All these new creation realities were loosed upon the creation when Jesus cried, "It is finished!" As the Jordan River of old was divided by the Ark of the Covenant, so God and not man completely and eternally rent the veil in the Temple from the top to the bottom when Jesus died. In the days of Joshua, the flood waters rolled back to the city of "Adam" (Josh. 3:16). Jesus, the true Ark, cut off every hindrance clear back to Genesis chapter 3 and the Fall of humankind!

Every 2,000 years, God has a "son"—Moses, then Jesus. Jesus was born in 4 B.C. We have just celebrated the year 2000 A.D. It is that time again in the earth! Jehovah married Israel in the Old Testament and had a Son—Messiah! Jesus has joined Himself to

His New Testament Bride and Wife. From that covenantal bond there now manifests another "son"—the third Son—the Manchild, the mature, overcoming remnant Church!

Chapter Four

The Third Son: The Manchild, the Mature Church

God begins His purposes with a man or woman, and then consummates His ultimate intention in and through a people or nation. Jehovah got together with His first anointed son at the burning bush. He then fulfilled His goal by delivering Israel, Moses' congregation, from the fleshpots of Egypt. The church in the wilderness was released from Pharaoh's tyranny to enjoy the full benefits and blessings of that inaugural Passover season.

Before time began, the Father established His eternal purpose in the Man Christ Jesus. The second Son was Heaven's corn of wheat who fell into earth's ground and died, then who came forth in resurrection and multiplication. Just as Moses' spirit was imparted to the 70 elders, God has now sent forth the Spirit of His Son into our hearts. Jesus became the firstborn among many brethren, the men and women who comprise His holy Nation, the glorious Church! We are His ongoing incarnation, the full expression and extension of the real Passover Lamb.

Gal. 4:19, KJV

My little children, of whom I travail in birth again until Christ be formed [fashioned] *in you.*

Gal. 4:19, TLB

...longing for the time when you will finally be filled with Christ.

Col. 1:27, KJV

To whom God would make known what is the riches of the glory of this mystery among the Gentiles [nations]; *which is Christ in you* [a plural pronoun], *the hope of glory.*

Every 2,000 years, God has a "son"—first Moses, then Jesus, and now the Manchild, the mature Church. This third Son is Christ fully formed in a people. My book, *Corporate Anointing* (Shippensburg, PA: Destiny Image, 1998) powerfully treats this truth that "Christ" is more than an individual. The anointed One of the New Covenant is both Head and Body, Jesus and His Church. We are the Body and Bride of Christ.

Moses wrestled with Pharaoh's stubbornness. Jesus was preserved from Herod's demonic wrath. The 21st century Church has been empowered to overcome the ancient serpent that became a great red dragon.

Moses' assembly bankrupted Egypt. Jesus rent the veil and released all things. The mature Church will arise and walk in all that Messiah died for! All creation awaits the manifestation and unveiling of *the* Son in and through a vast company of sons and daughters.

We are destined to understand, acknowledge, appropriate, *experience*, and then manifest the spoils of His eternal conquest in Gethsemane, on Calvary's cross, and at the empty tomb!

It is not simply an intellectual understanding of this truth that will guarantee an "entering" into the spiritual reality of this overcoming company. We must first internally experience the truth of "sonship" before we can externally manifest its living reality to the world.

Right now in many hidden places around the world an immeasurable company is being trained in the school of the Spirit. The nature of Christ is being woven into the fabric of their beings.

The process is tiresome and tedious, but the results will be stunning and spectacular. All of creation is on tiptoe in anxious anticipation of the dramatic display of this glorious spectacle—the corporate Man, the Manchild, sons of His love.

We are about to be fully delivered from the bondage and corruption of our "Egypt"—the slavery of sin and satan—and finally released into the freedom of the glory of the children of God!

This chapter finalizes the trilogy, fulfilling our prophetic model. This section completes the story of God's three "sons."

Rom. 8:19, KJV

For the earnest expectation of the creature waiteth for the manifestation of the sons of God.

Rom. 8:19-23, NIV

The creation waits in eager expectation for the sons of God to be revealed.

For the creation was subjected to frustration, not by its own choice, but by the will of the one who subjected it, in hope

that the creation itself will be liberated from its bondage to decay and brought into the glorious freedom of the children of God.

We know that the whole creation has been groaning as in the pains of childbirth right up to the present time.

Not only so, but we ourselves, who have the firstfruits of the Spirit, groan inwardly as we wait eagerly for our adoption as sons, the redemption of our bodies.

The word for "manifestation" in Romans 8:19 (KJV) is *apokalupsis* (Strong's #602), and it means, "a disclosure; a laying bare, making naked, manifestation, appearance; unveiling." Its verb form means "to take off the cover; to lay open what has been veiled or covered up; to make known, to make manifest." It is taken from *apo* ("away from") and *kalupto* ("to hide or cover"). The whole creation awaits the unveiling of God's third Son.

The Person—God's Chosen Deliverer

As were Moses and Jesus, so God's corporate Son, the mature Church, is a company of saviors, deliverers, peacemakers, and reconcilers, an interceding king-priest ministry. Moses mediated the law. Jesus propitiated grace and truth. The third Son will stand in the gap and make up the hedge—this is the corporate Man for whom God has sought (Ezek. 22:30).

Throughout the Scriptures, we see the pattern of a man, a maid, and a manchild. One classic Old Testament example of this is set forth in the story of the faith of the man Abraham, the restoration and rejuvenation of the maid Sarah, and the consequent birth of the manchild Isaac (whose name means "laughter"). Paul affirmed this connection to us believers in his letter to the Galatians, "Now we, brethren, as Isaac was, are the children of promise" (Gal. 4:28, KJV).

Two powerful passages in the last book of the Bible describe this Manchild, this promised third "son"—Revelation 12:1-5 and Revelation 14:1-5.

Rev. 12:1-5, KJV

And there appeared a great wonder in heaven; a woman clothed [all around] *with the sun, and the moon* [down] *under her feet, and upon her head a* [victor's] *crown of twelve stars:*

And she being with child cried, travailing in birth, and pained to be delivered.

And there appeared another wonder in heaven; and behold a great red [fire-like] dragon, having seven heads and ten horns, and seven crowns upon his heads.

And his tail drew the third part of the stars of heaven, and did cast them to the earth: and the dragon stood before the woman which was ready to be delivered [brought forth], for to devour [consume or swallow down] her child as soon as it was born.

And she brought forth a man child, who was to rule [shepherd] all nations with a rod of iron: and her child was caught up [suddenly seized or snatched] unto God, and to his throne.

This wonderful woman is the same woman who is mentioned in the fifth chapter of Ephesians. She is the Church, the Bride of Christ.

This woman of Revelation 12 cannot be natural Israel, for she appeared "in heaven." She is heavenly,[1] not earthy. She is the free-woman, a freeborn citizen, and not the bondwoman, a slave. She is the heavenly, not the earthly Jerusalem (Gal. 4:21-31). Much more could be said about this glorious Church, but for now we simply note that she is:

1. Clothed—The sun is the Son. This Church is in Christ.

2. Conquering—The moon can either represent the powers of darkness, or the Law. This Church has both under her feet.

3. Crowned—Twelve is the biblical number for government. This Church is walking in victory and divine order.

Gal. 4:19, KJV

My little children, of whom I travail in birth again until Christ be formed in you,

Gal. 4:19, TLB

Oh, my children, how you are hurting me! I am once again suffering for you the pains of a mother waiting for her child to be born—longing for the time when you will finally be filled with Christ.

Jochebed gave birth to Moses in the land of Egypt. Almost two thousand years later, the Virgin Mary brought forth Jesus in the shepherd's cave. At the dawning of this new century and millennium, another child of destiny, the third Son, is in the sun-clothed woman's womb, the "womb of the morning" (Ps. 110:3). John hears her crying aloud, travailing in birth pangs, "tortured with acute pains" to be delivered. This is the Greek word *basanos*, and it refers to a touchstone, which is a black siliceous stone used to test the purity of gold or silver by the color of the streak produced on it by rubbing it with either metal. When the woman's son is being birthed out, he will "come forth as gold" (symbolizing the divine nature) (Job 23:10 with 2 Pet. 1:4).

Rev. 12:5, KJV

And she brought forth a man child, who was to rule all nations with a rod of iron: and her child was caught up unto God, and to His throne.

Rev. 12:5, NIV

She gave birth to a son, a male child, who will rule all the nations with an iron scepter. And her child was snatched up to God and to His throne.

Ps. 2:8-9, NIV

Ask of Me, and I will make the nations Your inheritance, the ends of the earth Your possession.

You will rule them with an iron scepter...

God's third Son is a "man child," literally, "a son, a male." This *huios* or mature "son" is intended or destined to "rule" (*poimaino*, "to tend as a shepherd, to govern") all nations with "a rod (staff or scepter) of iron." This latter phrase describes an authority that will not yield or bend, and is primarily Messianic. Through the psalmist, this promised influence was first made by the Father to His Son

Jesus. By extension, it points to the authority given by King Jesus to the corporate Man created in His image.

Rev. 2:26-27, NIV

To him who overcomes and does My will to the end, I will give authority over the nations—

"He will rule them with an iron scepter; he will dash them to pieces like pottery"—just as I have received authority from My Father.

As John beheld this vision, the "man child" was "caught up" or "snatched up" to God and to His "throne" (the place or seat of royal authority and power). Thayer's Lexicon calls this "a throne seat, a chair of state having a footstool." The word for "caught up" in Revelation 12:5 (KJV) is *harpazo* (Strong's #726), and it means, "to seize, to carry off by force (suddenly exercised); to seize on, to claim for oneself eagerly; to snatch out or to snatch away." It is derived from the verb *haireomai*, which means, "to take for oneself, to prefer, to choose."

The biblical word *harpazo* is also used to describe the translation of Philip the evangelist from Gaza to Azotus; the catching up of Paul into the third heaven, into paradise (although the apostle never left the earth); and the seizing of the saints at the coming of the Lord (Acts 8:39; 2 Cor. 12:2-4; 1 Thess. 4:17).

We are describing God's third Son, His chosen Deliverer, the mature Church. The "man child" Company mentioned in Revelation 12:1-5 is further depicted as the 144,000 in Revelation 14:1-5. Note each verse, as rendered in the King James Version.

Rev. 14:1

And I looked, and, lo, a Lamb stood on the mount Sion, and with Him an hundred forty and four thousand, having His Father's name written in their foreheads.

The prevailing Lamb of the Book of Revelation is Jesus, the second Son, the Pattern Son. Mount Sion[2] is the Church of the first-born, the center of His king-priest ministry. The number 144,000 factors down into 12 times 12 times 1,000, and it speaks of the full stature of a governmental people. These overcomers had "His" (Jesus') Father's name written in "their" foreheads. The mind that was in Christ Jesus was the Father's mind—Paul admonished, "Let this mind be in you…" (Phil. 2:5). The third Son, the mature son, thinks like God.

Rev. 14:2

And I heard a voice from heaven, as the voice of many waters, and as the voice of a great thunder: and I heard the voice of harpers harping with their harps:

The voice of the third Son is a corporate voice, the voice of "many waters."[3] It is His voice of "thunder," the "roaring" of the Lion of Judah, symbolizing His power and might. It is the voice or sound of "harpers," players and singers filled with worship and praise, ministering the new song and the new sound for this new day.

Rev. 14:3

And they sung as it were a new song before the throne, and before the four beasts, and the elders: and no man could learn that song but the hundred and forty and four thousand, which were redeemed from the earth.

The final chapter of this writing will show that the song of the 144,000 is a "[fresh] new song"[4] that has never been sung before by anyone except Moses and the Lamb (Rev. 15:3). Our new song is by the Lord, from the Lord, about the Lord, and unto the Lord.

This new song is sung "before" or "in the face of, in the presence of" the throne. We have had to "learn [by use and practice]" this new song by the things which we have suffered (Eph. 4:20; Heb. 5:8,14), having been redeemed and separated "[away] from" the earth.

This "new song" is birthed out of pain and suffering. Heaven's lyrics are scratched on the linings of our souls as we learn about the faithfulness and grace of God in the fires of pain, persecution, and personal heartache.

Rev. 14:4

These are they which were not defiled with women; for they are virgins. These are they which follow the Lamb whithersoever He goeth. These were redeemed from among men, being the firstfruits unto God and to the Lamb.

The Manchild is pure, not "defiled" (soiled, polluted, contaminated, stained) with "women," or religious systems, as pictured in Proverbs 7 and Revelation 17-18. In unprecedented proportions, multitudes of God's people are crawling out of the dark cocoon of religious traditions and man-made systems. They are looking for the place of intimate relationship with the Father and longing to discover their position in His ultimate purposes.

The overcomer is a Virgin Church who "follows" (accompanies) the Lamb, the forerunner, into the Most Holy Place (Heb. 6:19-20). They are the "firstfruits" company of a great end-time harvest, having matured first. Joel prophesied that the former rain and the latter rain would be poured out in a people known as the "first" (Joel 2:23, KJV); the word *month* is in italics, having been supplied by the translators.

Rev. 14:5

And in their mouth was found no guile: for they are without fault before the throne of God.

These sons have no "guile," no "falsehood or untruth," in their mouths. This is the Man in the throne with the ministry of reconciliation, which operates by the power of the creative, spoken word. My book *The More Excellent Ministry* (Shippensburg, PA: Destiny Image, 1988) sets forth in depth this king-priest ministry after the order (manner, similitude) of Melchisedec (Heb. 5:1–8:6).

There we learn that this third corporate Son is a company of saviors, peacemakers, and reconcilers. We are being sent throughout the nations of the earth with the creative Word to forgive and to bless. Finally, these are without "fault" or "stain"—they are without blemish and faultless, like the Lamb whom they wholly follow!

Obad. 1:21, KJV

And saviours [liberators, victors, helpers] *shall come up on mount Zion to judge the mount of Esau; and the kingdom shall be the Lord's.*

Obad. 1:21, NIV

Deliverers will go up on Mount Zion to govern the mountains of Esau. And the kingdom will be the Lord's.

Mt. 5:9, KJV

Blessed are the peacemakers: for they shall be called the children [huioi, plural of huios, a "mature son"] *of God.*

2 Cor. 5:18-20, KJV

And all things are of God, who hath reconciled us to Himself by Jesus Christ, and hath given to us the ministry of reconciliation;

To wit, that God was in Christ, reconciling the world unto Himself, not imputing their trespasses unto them; and hath committed unto us the word of reconciliation.

Now then we are ambassadors [presbeuo, "seniors, elders, mature ones"] *for Christ, as though God did beseech you by us: we pray you in Christ's stead, be ye reconciled to God.*

This Manchild, this mature Church, is illustrated throughout the Scriptures. Three more of many key examples are a Joseph Company (Gen. 37–50), a David (or Judah) Company (1 Sam. 16–1 Kings 2), and Joel's Army (Joel 2). Bill Britton, a literary prophet who pioneered the message of sonship in America and the nations, was my close friend (from my first meeting him in 1980 until his death in 1985). Bill simply called this mature Church "the Overcomer."[5]

Rev 21:7, KJV

He that overcometh shall inherit all things; and I will be his God, and he shall be My son.

The Persecution—God's Chosen Adversary

Each of God's three sons faces a powerful opponent. Moses had to deal with Pharaoh. Jesus was rescued from the jealous frenzy of Herod the Great. The mature Church must overcome the great red, fire-breathing dragon.

Rom. 8:37, KJV

Nay, in all these things we are more than conquerors through Him that loved us.

2 Cor. 2:14, KJV

Now thanks be unto God, which always causeth us to triumph in Christ...

Remember, the primary reason for writing this volume is to encourage those who have been impregnated with the living Word, those who presently carry the prophetic burden of the Lord.

Our season of birthing and coming forth is being wrought by great pain and travail. This present path is treacherous, marked with great difficulty and pitfalls. This dragon is "red" or fire-like." But rejoice! Amongst all the "fiery darts of the wicked [one]," and through every "fiery trial" (Eph. 6:16; 1 Pet. 4:12), we are the victors and not the victims!

Rev. 12:11, KJV

And they overcame him [the dragon] *by the blood of the Lamb, and by the word of their testimony; and they loved not their lives unto the death.*

The "great dragon" is the "old [original, primeval] serpent, called the devil [accuser, slanderer], and satan [adversary], which deceiveth [led astray] the whole world" (Rev. 12:9). How did the ancient "serpent" of the Book of Genesis become a "great red dragon" by the time we get to the Book of Revelation?

Gen. 3:14, KJV

And the Lord God said unto the serpent, Because thou hast done this, thou art cursed above all cattle, and above every beast of the field; upon thy belly shalt thou go, and dust shalt thou eat all the days of thy life.

Is. 65:25, KJV

...and dust shall be the serpent's meat [food].

1 Cor. 15:47-49, RSV

The first man was from the earth, a man of dust; the second man is from heaven.

As was the man of dust, so are those who are of the dust; and as is the man of heaven, so are those who are of heaven.

Just as we have borne the image of the man of dust, we shall also bear the image of the man of heaven.

The first man Adam was "a man of dust." The second Man, the last Adam, is "the Lord from heaven" (KJV). There is no "second Adam," for the last Adam came to bring a lasting end to the first Adam! The King James Version says, "the first man Adam was made a living soul...The first man is of the earth, earthy..." (1 Cor. 15:45,47).

The whispering serpent has greatened into a bellowing dragon because Adam's race has made him what he is! The old nature of the old man is the only thing that the serpent can feed upon. Over the centuries, men and women have fed him, and his reputation has enlarged! The only place where satan can live and move and have his being is in the realm of soul, the minds of men and women. He feeds upon "dust," the serpent's food. The devil is not our problem—what we *think* about the devil is our problem!

Job 1:6-7, KJV

Now there was a day when the sons of God came to present themselves before the Lord, and Satan came also among them.

And the Lord said unto Satan, Whence comest thou? Then Satan answered the Lord, and said, From going to and fro in the earth, and from walking up and down in it.

As noted, God had pronounced judgment upon the serpent following the transgression in the Garden, "Upon thy belly shalt thou go..." Job is the oldest book in the Bible, but by the time it was written, someone had given satan some mobility. Someone had given him legs! Who did that? Men and women in their earthy ignorance "fed" him. The devil feeds upon "dust," the carnality of the first man Adam.

But God's third Son is in Christ, not Adam. The Greek rendering of First Corinthians 15:49 says of us, "And as we have borne the image of the earthy, so let us now put on and wear as a garment or a piece of armor the image of the heavenly." We are no longer men and women of the dust. Having been born of the Spirit, we are essentially spirit (Jn. 3:1-8; Heb. 12:9).

Gen. 3:19, KJV

...dust thou art, and unto dust shalt thou return.

1 Sam. 2:8, KJV

He raiseth up the poor out of the dust, and lifteth up the beggar from the dunghill, to set them among princes, and to make them inherit the throne of glory...

Is. 52:2, NIV

Shake off your dust; rise up, sit enthroned, O Jerusalem. Free yourself from the chains on your neck, O captive Daughter of Zion.

The new creation corporate Man has been raised up together, and made to sit together in heavenly places in Christ Jesus. Hear the

Word of the Lord to God's third Son, "Dust you were, but to dust you shall never return!" As did the Pattern Son Jesus, the Manchild out of the sun-clothed woman will by the corporate anointing ultimately put his feet on death itself.

There is a generation of whom Paul declared, "Behold, I show you a mystery. We shall not all sleep, but we shall all be changed, in a moment, in the twinkling of an eye, at the last trump: for the trumpet shall sound, and the dead shall be raised incorruptible, and we shall be changed. For this corruptible must put on incorruption, and this mortal must put on immortality" (1 Cor. 15:51-53, KJV).

Stop talking about the devil. Stop "feeding" him, lest the serpent grow into a dragon. Satan can only eat "dust." Be renewed in the spirit of your mind, and starve the devil to death! Beloved, shake off your dust. Rise up and sit enthroned in Christ!

Rev. 12:3-4, KJV

And there appeared another wonder in heaven; and behold a great red dragon, having seven heads and ten horns, and seven crowns upon his heads.

And his tail drew [dragged] *the third part of the stars of heaven, and did cast them to the earth: and the dragon stood before the woman which was* [about] *ready to be delivered* [bring forth], *for to devour* [eat down, consume] *her child as soon as it was born.*

The Greek word for this huge red (fire-like) "dragon" is *drakon*, and it is mentioned 12 times in John's Apocalypse.[6] This number reveals the governmental structure and order of the kingdom of darkness (Eph. 6:11-12). Vine's Dictionary says that *drakon* denotes "a mythical monster, a dragon"; "a large serpent, so called because of its keen power of sight" (from a root *derk*, signifying "to see").

This is not the time or the place to discuss the dragon's "seven heads and ten horns." Suffice it to say that John uses this same phrase to describe the great red dragon, the beast that rises up out of the sea, and the woman (the mother of harlots) riding the back of the scarlet-colored beast (Rev. 12:3; 13:1; 17:1-5). One other brief thought—Isaiah shows us that the dragon's "tail" is "the prophet that teacheth lies" (Is. 9:15).

Rev. 12:7-11, KJV

And there was war in heaven: Michael[7] and his angels fought against the dragon; and the dragon fought and his angels,

And prevailed not; neither was their place found any more in heaven.

And the great dragon was cast out, that old serpent, called the devil, and satan, which deceiveth the whole world: he was cast out into the earth, and his angels were cast out with him.

And I heard a loud voice saying in heaven, Now is come salvation, and strength, and the kingdom of our God, and the power of His Christ: for the accuser of our brethren is cast down, which accused them before our God day and night.

And they overcame him by the blood of the Lamb, and by the word of their testimony; and they loved not their lives unto the death.

It is not our intent to fully exegete these passages, but rather to highlight their truth. Consider Revelation 12:7-11 in the light of the following prophetic Scriptures.

Ps. 74:13-14, KJV

Thou didst divide the sea by Thy strength: Thou brakest the heads of the dragons [Pharaoh's captains] *in the waters.*

Thou brakest the heads of leviathan in pieces, and gavest him to be meat to the people inhabiting the wilderness.

Is. 27:1, KJV

In that day the Lord with his sore and great and strong sword [Jesus, the Word of God] *shall punish leviathan the piercing serpent, even leviathan that crooked serpent; and He shall slay the dragon that is in the sea* [masses of unregenerate humanity].

Is. 51:9, KJV

Awake, awake, put on strength, O arm of the Lord; awake, as in the ancient days, in the generations of old. Art Thou not it that hath cut Rahab [Egypt], *and wounded the dragon* [of the Nile]?

Ezek. 29:3, KJV

Speak, and say, Thus saith the Lord GOD; Behold, I am against thee, Pharaoh king of Egypt, the great dragon that lieth in the midst of his rivers, which hath said, My river is mine own, and I have made it for myself.

First of all, these verses affirm Jehovah's historic subjugation of Pharaoh (pictured by leviathan or the dragon) in the days of His first son Moses. As noted in Chapter Two, this conquest points ahead to Jesus' total victory over the devil, the crooked serpent. The thought of Jesus slaying the dragon is fully treated in Chapter Two of my book *Whose Right It Is* (Shippensburg, PA: Destiny Image, 1995).

Satan "prevailed not" (Rev. 12:8, KJV). This word *ischuo* reveals that the evil one was not strong, was not a force, could not wield power, and had no strength to overcome. The word for "place" in the same verse is *topos* ("a spot or space; a condition or opportunity;" English, "topography"), and is used in Paul's admonition in the King James Version of Ephesians 4:27, "Neither give place to the devil."

The second Son, the Pattern Son, is the Dragon-slayer! The third Son has begun to appropriate His eternal victory. King David slew the Philistine champion Goliath; then David's mighty men slew Goliath's kinfolk (1 Sam. 17; 1 Chron. 20). Jesus defeated satan, and His mature Church has been called to rid the earth of satan's influence. The authority of "Christ"—the Anointed One and His anointing in and through a people—will manifest salvation, strength (joy), and the Kingdom of God throughout the earth!

Rev. 12:11, NIV

> *They overcame him by the blood of the Lamb and by the word of their testimony; they did not love their lives so much as to shrink from death.*

Moses and his church witnessed the demise of Pharaoh and his army at the Red Sea. Jesus Christ overcame the world, the flesh, and the devil (Jn. 16:33; Rev. 3:21). The mature Church overthrows the great red dragon by His blood. The shed blood of the Passover Lamb gives us a right to speak, and the word of our testimony now goes forth, even in the face of death! We love not our "lives," our "souls" (intellect, emotions, and will—what we think, feel and want). This is our day, our season, and we are not afraid.

The Passover Principle—God's Chosen Season

Lk. 22:15-16, KJV

> *And He said unto them, With desire I have desired to eat this passover with you before I suffer:*
>
> *For I say unto you, I will not any more eat thereof, until it be fulfilled in the kingdom of God.*

Moses inaugurated the Passover. Jesus was the slain Lamb who took away the sin of the world. The third Son, empowered by His Spirit, is about to experience the Passover of the Kingdom as we pass over into another age. The bloody Paschal paradigm moves on through the Bible, saturating the prophetic cycle of God's three sons.

Lev. 23:18, KJV

> *And ye shall offer with the bread seven lambs without blemish of the first year...*

Rev. 5:5-6, KJV

*...behold, the Lion of the tribe of Juda, the Root of
David, hath prevailed to open the book, and to loose the
seven seals thereof.*

*And I beheld, and, lo, in the midst of the throne and
of the four beasts, and in the midst of the elders, stood a
Lamb as it had been slain, having seven horns and seven
eyes, which are the seven Spirits of God sent forth into all
the earth.*

The Holy Spirit of the New Testament Passover Lamb is revealed in seven dimensions, denoting the fullness of the Lamb. Jesus
was anointed with the Spirit without measure (Jn. 3:34). The "seven
lambs" of Leviticus 23:18 point to His "seven horns" (all power and
authority), and His "seven eyes" (complete understanding).

The Pattern Son will have a people who will have come to the
fullness of His stature and character, a vast family of sons conformed to the image of the Firstborn. Jesus is the true Vine and we
are His branches, the Lamb's kin (Jn. 15:1-5). The mature Church
partakes of His divine nature and the fullness of His Holy Spirit, the
sevenfold anointing that Isaiah prophesied would rest on Messiah
(see the next section of this chapter below). John saw this as "the
seven spirits of God," the seven lamps before the throne (see Rev.
1:4; 3:1; 4:5; 5:6). This anointing is ultimately "sent" (*apostello*)
with great apostolic authority into all the earth! The writer to the
Hebrews vividly described this seven-branched Lampstand.

Heb. 2:10-13, KJV

For it became [was fitting for] *Him, for whom are all
things, and by whom are all things, in bringing many sons
unto glory, to make the captain of their salvation perfect
through sufferings.*

*For both He that sanctifieth and they who are sancti-
fied are all of one: for which cause He is not ashamed to
call them brethren,*

Saying, I will declare Thy name unto My brethren, in the midst of the church will I sing praise unto Thee.

And again, I will put My trust in Him. And again, Behold I and the children which God hath given Me.

The writer quotes Psalms 22:22,25 and Isaiah 8:18 in this passage. In Hebrews 2:11, he uses a Greek ablative of source. Jesus and His brothers are all "of" (*ek*, "out of") the same source. This pictures the Golden Candlestick (Lampstand) in the Mosaic Tabernacle, made without a manmade mold, and fashioned or beaten out of one piece of pure gold (Ex. 25:31,37,39). The New American Standard Version for Hebrews 2:11 says that they are "all from one Father"; the New International Version declares that they are "of the same family." The Revised Standard Version says that the Elder Brother and His seed "have all one origin."

A similar Old Testament parallel is Zechariah's powerful prophecy about the "two olive trees" that flank the Candlestick, the two "anointed ones," literally, the two "sons of oil" (Zech. 4:10-14). Again, "seven lambs" point to the "seven Spirits of God"—the fullness of the Spirit of the Lamb.

All three of God's sons—Moses, Jesus, and the Manchild—experience the chosen season of the Passover lamb. The eight specific provisions for the Passover ordinance, and how they played out in the lives of the first two "sons," were given in Chapters Two and Three (Ex. 12:1-23). We now apply those same truths to the third Son, the corporate Man, the mature Church:

First, the people selected a lamb, a kid without blemish, for each household on the tenth of the month. God's end-time, mature ones were chosen out and apprehended before we were born and before we were saved. A domestic principle unfolds when we discover that it was the responsibility of the man to provide the lamb for his household.

Eph 1:4, KJV

*According as He hath chosen us in Him before the
foundation of the world, that we should be holy and without blame before Him in love.*

Second, they killed the lamb on the 14th of Abib at evening. It
had to be inspected for four days to ensure its purity. The Lamb
(Jesus) was killed for each of us. His killing was my killing.
His death was my death. Pristine Christianity is the replaced
life, living by the life of Another.

Gal. 2:20, NAS

*I have been crucified with Christ; and it is no longer
I who live, but Christ lives in me; and the {life} which I
now live in the flesh I live by faith in the Son of God, who
loved me, and gave Himself up for me.*

Third, the people dipped a bunch of hyssop in the blood, and
then sprinkled the side posts and the upper doorpost, forming
two crosses. This "double cross" was a twofold witness of their
blood covenant with God (vertically), and their blood covenant
with man (horizontally). Because there is blood on the "Door"
(Jesus called Himself the "Door" in John 10:9), His third "son"
is protected with a spiritual immunity! Fear not, for the Lamb
will save you. His blood will never lose its power. Death and
hell must pass by. They cannot abide here, for you and yours
are the property of Another.

Lk. 10:19, NKJ

*Behold, I give you the authority to trample on ser-
pents and scorpions, and over all the power of the enemy,
and nothing shall by any means hurt you.*

Fourth, they roasted the whole animal, without a broken bone,
with fire. The lamb was not to be eaten raw nor sodden with
water. It was completely consumed (including the head as well
as legs and innards). One lamb was eaten by each family,
including slaves and strangers, if they were circumcised. If
the number of the family was too small, they might join a

neighboring family. This fourth principle cannot be watered down. Be consumed with His head (His mind), His legs (His mobility), and His "inward parts" (His motives). The Manchild, the mature Church, eats the "whole" Lamb:

a. We are a Temple of whole stones (Deut. 27:6; 1 Pet. 2:5).

b. We are a whole burnt offering (Ps. 51:19; Rom. 12:1-2).

c. We seek God with our "whole heart" (Ps. 119:2,10,34,58,69,145).

d. We have a single eye, a whole body full of light (Mt. 6:22-23).

e. We have put on the whole armor of God (Eph. 6:10-18).

1 Thess. 5:23, KJV

And the very God of peace sanctify you wholly; and I pray God your whole spirit and soul and body be preserved blameless unto the coming of our Lord Jesus Christ.

Fifth, the people ate the Passover lamb with unleavened bread and bitter herbs. Unleavened bread is squeezed or compressed bread, made heavy without leaven, or yeast. The Lamb comes with a side dish, the bitter herbs—a lifestyle of repentance, the constant renewing of the mind. Repentance is an attitude, a way of life for the third Son, the mature Church. It operates in two tracks: personal relationships and personal evangelism. The overcomer's life is one of holiness, marked by the bittersweet fellowship of His suffering.

1 Cor. 5:7-8, NAS

Clean out the old leaven so that you may be a new lump, just as you are {in fact} unleavened. For Christ our Passover also has been sacrificed.

Therefore let us celebrate the feast, not with old leaven, nor with the leaven of malice and wickedness, but with the unleavened bread of sincerity and truth.

Sixth, the people ate the Paschal meal. The overcoming Church is invited to "eat His flesh" and "drink His blood."

John 6:56, NAS

"He who eats My flesh and drinks My blood abides in Me, and I in him."

At this point in His ministry and with these strange words, Jesus draws a line in the sand. He already had thousands of followers, but this would be a defining moment for each one of them.

A decision would have to be made. He was calling them to a deeper commitment that involved much more than fascination with "signs and wonders" and the scintillation of mystic truths.

Jesus said that His meat was to do the will of His Father. Our Paschal celebration includes clearing the table of the scraps of fanciful teachings and traditional rhetoric. We must replace it with the Passover meal of the rich food that comes from the mouth of the Father, delivered to us by the power of the Holy Spirit. This new diet of the "will of the Father" is true kingdom food that will mature the corporate man.

> The people ate the Paschal meal in haste, with their loins girded, with shoes on their feet, and a staff in their hand, ready to leave Egypt. The mature Church has put on Christ, the garment of salvation. Our strength is in Him. Our feet are shod with the whole armor of God. As noted, the Overcomer is destined to shepherd the nations with a rod and staff of iron. These principles picture our preparedness and "readiness of mind" to walk with God (Acts 17:11). Are you "ready"?[8]

Eph. 6:14-15, KJV

Stand therefore, having your loins girt about with truth, and having on the breastplate of righteousness;

And your feet shod with the preparation of the gospel of peace.

Seventh, the people remained in the house until the morning, staying obediently under the covenantal protection of the blood. Be like the love-slave with the pierced ear who chooses to stay with the Master and His family (Ex. 21:1-6). Stay in the House, the local church. Stay with seasoned father and mother ministry. Stay with the family. Stay in this journey for the long haul, until the full dawning of this new day. This is a serious season. It's dangerous to go outside before daybreak—there is a lion in the streets (Prov. 26:13; 1 Pet. 5:8)! The "destroyer" is on the loose (Ex. 12:23; Jn. 10:10; 1 Cor. 10:10).

Gen. 32:24, KJV

And Jacob was left alone; and there wrestled a man with him until the breaking of the day.

Song 4:6, KJV

Until the day break, and the shadows flee away, I will get me to the mountain of myrrh, and to the hill of frankincense.

Finally, they burned all of the Passover lamb that remained, for it could only be eaten during the night. None was to remain until the morning (dawn, daybreak). Whatever part of the lamb could not be eaten was to be burned the next morning. Nothing of it was to be carried out of the house. This was done primarily to prevent putrefaction. A thing offered to God should not be subjected to corruption or decay. The Manchild, the mature Church, will put on incorruption and immortality.

1 Cor. 15:53-55, KJV

For this corruptible must put on incorruption, and this mortal must put on immortality.

So when this corruptible shall have put on incorruption, and this mortal shall have put on immortality, then shall be brought to pass the saying that is written, Death is swallowed up in victory.

O death, where is thy sting? O grave, where is thy victory?

Moses, God's first son, kept God's word concerning the Passover by faith. Jesus Christ strode to Calvary fully persuaded that the Father would raise Him from the dead on the third day (Mt. 16:21; 17:23; 20:19). Consequently, He became the Author and the Finisher of the faith of the third Son!

> Do we know the voice? Can we be led by the voice? Have we the faith that can follow when the path seems so strangely crooked? There must be such a clear conception of the Lord, together with the cultivated habit of recognizing His gentlest intimation, and obeying it without question. It is a splendid abandonment to the will of another, which has been called a "holy recklessness," as to consequences. It may oppose human reason and circumstances, but if He calls—FOLLOW—....[9]

The mature Church walks by His faith, not by our sight, knowing that God's day begins in the evening and ends in the morning (Gen. 1:5). Things don't have to be perfectly clear, and we don't have to have all the answers. We follow the Lord because we love Him, and because we are fully convinced that "he that cometh to God must believe that He is, and that He is a rewarder of them that diligently seek Him" (Heb. 11:6).

The Passover is God's chosen season. The Greek word for "Hebrews" means "to cross over, to pass over, to cross the river." The mature Church has been brought out of Egypt, through the wilderness, and has now entered into the land. We have been baptized into Moses at the Red Sea (water baptism) and in the cloud (Holy Ghost baptism) (1 Cor. 10:1-4, 11).

The time has come for our *third* baptism—into Joshua at the Jordan River. We are the generation who will "cross the river." As noted earlier, every hindrance clear back to "Adam" has been cut off (Josh. 3:16), and every blessing in heavenly places in Christ Jesus has been released!

The Provision—God's Chosen Transfer of Wealth (Health and Blessing)

Moses and his church received all their back wages at once. At Calvary, Jesus redeemed and recovered all things, once for all. All that has been written and all that has happened is for the people upon whom the ends of the ages have come (1 Cor. 10:11)!

In the original Exodus, God's first son and his congregation came out of Egypt with unparalleled wealth. None was feeble among them. When Jesus experienced His "exodus" at the cross, He left this world and led captivity captive. As a baby, preserved from Herod's wrath, our Lord was called "out of Egypt" (Hos. 11:1; Mt. 2:15). The Manchild, the mature Church, follows the ongoing pattern. We who have been called "out of Egypt" are:

1. A worshiping people (Ex. 3:12).

2. A militant people (Ex. 12:51).

3. A disciplined people (Ex. 13:10).

4. A liberated people (Ex. 20:2).

5. A holy people (Lev. 11:45).

6. An honest people (Lev. 19:36).

7. A fruitful people (Ps. 80:8).

8. A remnant people (Is. 11:11).

9. A covenantal people (Jer. 31:32).

2 Pet. 1:3-4, KJV

According as His [the Lamb's] *divine power hath given unto us all things that pertain unto life and godliness, through the knowledge of Him that hath called us to glory and virtue:*

Whereby are given unto us exceeding great and precious promises: that by these ye might be partakers of the divine nature, having escaped the corruption that is in the world through lust.

As noted in Chapter Two, every miraculous provision and blessing of health and wealth that came upon Moses and his church in the wilderness took place for one reason—they had obediently eaten the lamb! How much more for us New Testament believers who have left our "Egypt," all that is in the world (1 Jn. 2:15-17). We are partakers of Christ, of the Lamb's divine power and nature!

The Feast of Tabernacles is a global harvest, impacting every nation of the earth. Isaiah in the Old Testament and John in the New Testament caught glimpses of the health, wealth, and blessing that are the worthy portion, the double portion, of God's third Son. As you take time to read, study, and meditate our brief exegesis of these timeless passages, reflect on how blessed you are just to be alive in this awesome moment of God's unfolding purpose.

There is a God. God has a plan. That plan is always working. And that plan includes you!

Is. 60:1-5, KJV

Arise, shine [be radiant]*; for thy light is come, and the glory of the Lord is risen upon thee* [quoted in Eph. 5:14].

For, behold, the darkness [misery, destruction, death, ignorance, sorrow, wickedness] *shall cover the earth, and gross darkness* [thick gloom] *the people: but the Lord shall arise* [like the sun] *upon thee, and His glory shall be seen upon thee.*

And the Gentiles [the nations] *shall come to thy light, and kings to the brightness* [brilliancy] *of thy rising.*

Lift up thine eyes round about, and see: all they gather themselves together, they come to thee: thy sons shall come from far, and thy daughters shall be nursed [supported, confirmed; this is *aman*, the word for "faith"] *at thy side* [these are the "kings" of verse 3, as prophesied in Gen. 17:6].

Then thou shalt see, and flow [stream—Is. 2:2; Jer. 31:12] *together, and thine heart shall fear* [reverence], *and be enlarged* [broadened]*; because the abundance of the sea* [wealth of a multitude] *shall be converted* [turned over] *unto thee, the forces* [of men, means, or other resources] *of the Gentiles* [nations] *shall come unto thee.*

Is. 60:5, NAS

Then you will see and be radiant, and your heart will thrill and rejoice; because the abundance of the sea will be turned to you, the wealth of the nations will come to you.

Rev. 21:23-24, KJV

And the city had no need of the sun, neither of the moon, to shine in it: for the glory of God did lighten it, and the Lamb is the light thereof.

And the nations of them which are saved shall walk in the light of it: and the kings of the earth do bring their glory [splendor, magnificence] *and honour* [valuables] *into it.*

Rev. 22:1-2, KJV

And he showed me a pure [clean] *river of water of life, clear* [*lampros*, the word for "shining, radiant, transparent, or brilliant"] *as crystal* [precious stone]*, proceeding* [issuing] *out of the throne of God and of the Lamb.*

In the midst of the street [the broad way] *of it, and on either side of the river, was there the tree of life, which bare* [made] *twelve manner of fruits, and yielded* [gave away] *her fruit every month: and the leaves* [from *phule*, the word for "offshoot; race or clan"] *of the tree were for the healing* [curing] *of the nations.*

There are many other Scriptures that predict the massive transfer of wealth from the world to the Church in these end times.

Job 27:16-17, TLB

The evil man may accumulate money like dust, with closets jammed full of clothing—

yes, he may order them made by his tailor, but the innocent shall wear that clothing and shall divide his silver among them.

Prov. 13:22, KJV

...the wealth of the sinner is laid up for the just.

Prov. 28:8, NIV

He who increases his wealth by exorbitant interest amasses it for another, who will be kind to the poor.

Eccles. 2:26, NIV

To the man who pleases Him, God gives wisdom, knowledge and happiness, but to the sinner He gives the task of gathering and storing up wealth to hand it over to the one who pleases God...

The Manchild, the third Son, is mightily anointed by God to receive this abundance of health and wealth. King David was anointed three times (1 Sam. 16:13; 2 Sam. 2:4; 5:3). With his first anointing, David killed a bear, a lion, and the giant Goliath. Second, he was anointed by the tribe of Judah (which means "praise"). Third, he was anointed with full kingly authority by all the elders of Israel. The mature Church will walk in all three anointings, discussed in depth in Chapter Two of my book *Corporate Anointing* (Shippensburg, PA: Destiny Image, 1998).

An anointing (only God) has brought us out of Egypt and through the wilderness, which represent our childhood and adolescence in the things of the Spirit. Now we are postured to cross the river and enter the land (picturing our maturity in Christ). There is a third anointing that is presently bringing us in. The psalmist described this third operation of the Spirit as "fresh oil."

Ps. 92:10, KJV

*...I shall be anointed with **fresh oil**.*

The Hebrew word for "fresh" is *rah-an-awn* (Strong's #7488), and it means, "to be green; verdant; by analogy, new; figuratively, prosperous." This word is used 20 times in the Old Testament, and is translated once as "flourishing" in Psalm 92:14. Its primary meaning is given 18 times in the King James Version as "green."[10] This "fresh" oil is "green" oil. Green is the color of life, resurrection life (*zoe* life or divine life).

Psa 92:12-14, KJV

The righteous shall flourish like the palm tree: he shall grow like a cedar in Lebanon.

Those that be planted in the house of the Lord shall flourish in the courts of our God.

They shall still bring forth fruit in old age; they shall be fat and flourishing.

God lives in a "three-room House"—the divine pattern revealed in the Tabernacle of Moses.

The third room (compare the Third Day in God)—the Most Holy Place—is the living room (Jn. 14:6), and the loving room (1 Cor. 13:13).

The third room is also the "green" room!

Song 1:16, KJV

"Behold, thou art fair, my beloved, yea, pleasant: also our bed is green."

Rev. 4:3, KJV

And He that sat was to look upon like a jasper and a sardine stone: and there was a rainbow round about the throne, in sight like unto an [green] emerald."

David's three anointings further illustrate this (1 Sam. 16:13; 2 Sam. 2:4; 5:3). God's anointing has brought the Church out of Egypt and through the wilderness. The One who brought us out is about to bring us in (Deut. 6:23). Israel was brought out of Egypt by the hand of the shepherd Moses, then brought into Canaan by the word (command) of the soldier Joshua. The Ark split the Jordan in Joshua 3-4, upheld by a team of four priests—another picture of this corporate anointing. We have been freed, then filled, and are about to experience the fulfillment of the promised vision and inheritance!

The third anointing (which gave King David complete domin-ion over all Israel) for the third day[11] is the corporate anointing for the corporate, many-membered Man![12] This third anointing will sanction and empower God's third Son to possess the land. It per-fects (matures) the Church in the Most Holy Place—the spiritual bedroom and the throne room. The third anointing is "fresh" oil or "green" oil for the green room!

1 Pet. 2:9, KJV

But ye are a chosen generation, a royal priesthood, an holy nation...

Rev. 1:6, KJV

And hath made us kings and priests unto God...

Rev. 5:10, KJV

And hast made us unto our God kings and priests: and we shall reign on the earth.

This third "fresh oil" anointing will manifest throughout the Body of Christ as a fresh desire, a fresh energy, and a fresh ability in two principal dimensions:

First, we are priests unto God. This is the principle of brideship, bridal affection. This is fresh oil for the spiritual bedroom, which is for our intimacy with God. We are receiving a fresh desire, energy, and ability for prayer, praise, worship, and priestly obedience!

Second, we are kings unto men. This is the principle of sonship and inheritance. This is fresh oil for the throne room, which is for our dominion with God. We are receiving a fresh desire, energy, and ability to walk in a lifestyle marked by real miracles, power with God and men, and dominion in the earth!

Both Moses and Aaron, who picture this king-priest ministry, typify this anointed third Son. However, to stay with our pattern, we note both offices in Moses alone. The priestly aspect of unparalleled mercy was demonstrated in Moses' intercession for his people. The rod of Moses, which became the rod of God, confirmed the kingly side of unprecedented authority. Both points were introduced in Chapter Two.

Especially consider the Church's kingly authority, prefigured by the principle of Moses' "rod." It is awesome to think about the kind of power and authority given to Moses by God. The words of Moses and Aaron brought the tribulation of ten plagues to Egypt. Moses' "rod" denoted the authority of a father ministry. Father Moses taught Israel the fear of the Lord, becoming a "god" unto Ramses (Ex. 7:1).

Jesus, the second Son, the Pattern Son, has been given all authority in Heaven and on earth (Mt. 28:18). His power over death, His resurrection, was typified by Aaron's "rod" that budded at the time of Korah's rebellion (Num. 16-17).

The third Son, the Manchild, personifies the "rod." The rod of Aaron that budded is a picture of this firstfruits company unto God and the Lamb, previously set forth in Revelation 14:1-5. We are being energized by "the power of an endless life" (Heb. 7:16), the resurrection power of Jesus Christ. This people, like the branches that sprang out of the central shaft of the Golden Candlestick, come forth from the loins of the Lord and are His "seed"[13] (the 42nd "generation" of Matthew, chapter 1).

Aaron's rod that budded in the morning (a new day) is the emblem of God's chosen priesthood (1 Pet. 2:9-10), and presents many truths:

1. The rod is the scepter of a kingdom, and represents authority.

2. The rod is a shepherd's staff by which the flock is governed.

3. The rod is a "branch" (see below).

4. The rod is an instrument of correction.[14]

Is. 11:1-2, KJV

And there shall come forth a rod [Jesus] *out of the stem* [David] *of Jesse, and a Branch* [the third Son, the mature Church] *shall grow out of His roots:*

*And the spirit of the Lord shall rest upon **Him*** [the corporate Man, Christ the Head and Christ the Body], *the spirit of wisdom and understanding, the spirit of counsel and might, the spirit of knowledge and of the fear of the Lord.*

Is. 11:1, NIV

A shoot will come up from the stump of Jesse; from his roots a Branch will bear fruit.

Zech. 6:12, KJV

And speak unto him, saying, Thus speaketh the Lord of hosts, saying, Behold the [corporate] *man whose name is The **Branch**...*

The third Son, the mature Son, is the many-membered "branch"[15] of the Lord. The "Him" of Isaiah 11:2 prefigures the many-membered "new man" and "perfect (mature) man" of Ephesians 2:15; 4:13,24—this is the same mature Man as "he [or him] that overcometh" as set forth in the second and third chapters of the Book of Revelation.

Acts 17:31, NAS

Because He has fixed a day in which He will judge the world in righteousness through a Man whom He has appointed...

1 Cor. 6:2, TLB

Don't you know that someday we Christians are going to judge and govern the world? So why can't you decide even these little things among yourselves?

The Spirit "without measure" rested upon Jesus, the Pattern Son (Jn. 3:34). We have already noted in this chapter that this sevenfold anointing (pictured by the Lampstand and enumerated in Isaiah 11:2) will rest upon a governmental people. This fullness of the Spirit, revealed in the first five chapters of the Book of Revelation as "the seven Spirits of God," has many aspects (see Rev. 1:4; 3:1; 4:5; 5:6):

1. Seven spirits—one Spirit.

2. Seven lamps—fullness of illumination.

3. Seven horns—all power and authority.

4. Seven eyes—all-seeing, all understanding.

5. Seven colors—the rainbow around the throne; covenant. Compare Joseph's (ruler's) coat of many colors (Gen. 37).

Ps. 75:6-7, KJV

For promotion [to be high or exalted] *cometh neither from the east, nor from the west, nor from the south.*

But God is the judge: He putteth down one, and setteth up another.

Mal. 3:17, AMP

And they shall be Mine, says the Lord of hosts, in that day when I publicly recognize {and} openly declare them to be My jewels (My special possession, My peculiar treasure). And I will spare them, as a man spares his own son who serves him.

Mt. 17:5, KJV

While he yet spake, behold, a bright cloud overshadowed them: and behold a voice out of the cloud, which said, This is My beloved Son, in whom I am well pleased; hear ye Him.

Promotion does not come from the east, the west, or the south. Spiritual advancement comes from the north, out of Zion. Real promotion, Heaven's endorsement, comes from God. Men and women do not have to push themselves forward, because their gift will make room for their greatness (Prov. 18:16). The time for God to publicly recognize and openly declare His third Son is upon us.

Joseph is about to come out of prison. David is about to leave the cave. John the Baptist is about to walk out from the back side of the desert. Paul is about to leave Arabia and go up to Jerusalem to meet the leading brethren.

Yet it seems that men and women in America cannot wait for God's affirmation. Many are obsessed with titles, and make much to-do about setting themselves forward, craving and clamoring for recognition. We have no lack of bishops, apostles, and prophets. Family feuds have erupted over the petty issue of the seating arrangement on the convention platform. How sad. How sick.

Be patient, brothers and sisters. The Father is about to speak from Heaven as He affirms His jewels. Then everyone (who is in tune with His voice by the Spirit within) will know and appreciate who you are.

Neh. 7:73, KJV

So the priests, and the Levites, and the porters, and the singers, and some of the people, and the Nethinims, and all Israel, dwelt in their cities; and when the seventh month came, the children of Israel were in their cities.

Lk. 2:6-7, KJV

> *And so it was, that, while they were there, the days were accomplished that she should be delivered.*
>
> *And she brought forth her firstborn son...*

Every 2,000 years, God has a "son." History has repeated itself. Once again, as in the second chapter of Luke, the whole world is being taxed. The whole creation is groaning under the load. This God-appointed burden is driving every man and woman to his or her prearranged place of spiritual nativity. We are pregnant with vision, and our predetermined destiny is about to come forth.

It was not an easy journey for Mary and Joseph. But Caesar's decree, predicated by Micah's ancient prophecy (Mic. 5:2), prodded and pushed them on to Bethlehem, to the place—the only place—where Jesus could be born. It was *there*—not Nazareth, or Jerusalem, or any other place—it was "there" that the second Son, Mary's "firstborn son," uttered His first earthly cry!

Make your calling and election sure (2 Pet. 1:10). Make "sure" that you are in the *place* and with the *people* among whom your "baby"—your foreordained destiny—is to be birthed and come forth. You will not have your "baby" any other way. The seventh month has arrived, the time for the Feast of Tabernacles and the manifestation of God's third Son. Are you in your city? Are you and your family fleshing out meaningful relationships among your people? Your destiny can only be fulfilled "there."

Every 2,000 years, God has a "son"...

We have come full circle, having meditated on the wonder of God's three "sons." The continuity of their pattern has been steady as we have made known and contemplated each story:

1. His person as God's *chosen deliverer*.

2. His times of persecution at the hands of a *chosen adversary*.

3. His sharing the *chosen season* of the Passover paradigm.

4. The blessings he and his people have received as God's *chosen provision*.

There remains one final thread of continuity and commonality among this "threefold cord," this cord of three strands, that is not quickly or easily broken (Eccles. 4:12). All three "sons" have a song to sing!

Song 2:11-12, KJV

For, lo, the winter is past, the rain is over and gone;

The flowers appear on the earth; the time of the singing of birds is come, and the voice of the turtle is heard in our land;

Song 2:12, TLB

The flowers are springing up and the time of the singing of birds has come. Yes, spring is here.

Chapter Five

Sing, O Barren

Is. 54:1, KJV

Sing, O barren, thou that didst not bear; break forth into singing, and cry aloud, thou that didst not travail with child...

Every 2,000 years, God has a "son."

Each is God's chosen deliverer. Each is challenged by God's chosen adversary. Each experiences the Passover, God's chosen season. Each receives God's chosen transfer of health, wealth, and favored blessings.

Moreover, each "son" is birthed out of barrenness.

Moses appeared after four barren centuries of captivity and slavery. Jesus was generated from the epitome of a barren womb— the virgin womb of Mary! The Manchild, the mature Church, is about to be manifested out from many empty, frustrating years of seeming barrenness.

Before there can be a birth, of necessity there must be a union. Then out of that spiritual union will come forth the son of prom- ise. The corporate man will come forth amidst great pain and suf- fering. But out of that suffering a song is created whose melody will fill the earth.

Secrets of Union[1]

Union with God is not a philosophic theory or a pursuit of religious experiences. It is nothing less than the union of man's spirit with the God of the Universe.

The spiritual experiences of man are only the "raw material" that awakens a love and a longing for Him. Man is easily mesmerized with these encounters, and the temptation is to camp around these spiritual sightings.

Union is that perfect and self-forgetting harmony of the regenerate will of man with his God. It makes the soul of man become to the Eternal God what the hand is to the body. Inflamed by a child-like, fiery love, we no longer are concerned with our own selfish interests. We seek solely the honor and glory of our Father. Union with God means that all of the stirrings of the heart are beating in a synchronous movement with the rhythm of the divine.

The supreme summit of this union is not an achieved condition of stillness, nor a blank absorption in the absolute. Rather it is a life so rich and so abundant that it requires for its expression the extremes of activity and rest, pouring itself out in generous acts of charity to all and yet inwardly abiding in unbroken rest. This union can only be discovered in the third room of the House of God, the Most Holy Place, the loving room.

You will ask, then—how, since His track is traceless, can I know that He is present? The answer is that He is living and full of energy, and as soon as He has entered me, He quickens my sleeping soul. He begins to pluck up and destroy, plant and build, to water the dry places, light up the dark places, throw open what was shut, inflame with warmth what was cold, straighten the crooked path, and make rough places smooth. I can feel His movements within me calling me towards a holy marriage where my life is consumed in Him.

In the reformation and renewal of the spirit of my mind—that is, my inward man—I have seen something of the loveliness of His beauty. Meditating on these things, I have been filled with wonder at the multitude of His greatness. But when the Word withdrew, all these spiritual powers and faculties began to droop and languish, as if the fire were taken from beneath a bubbling pot; and this is to me the sign of His departure. Then my soul must be sad and sorry, till He comes back and my heart again warms within me.

Jn. 15:4-5, NAS

"Abide in Me, and I in you. As the branch cannot bear fruit of itself, unless it abides in the vine, so neither can you unless you abide in Me.

"I am the vine, you are the branches; he who abides in Me, and I in him, he bears much fruit, for apart from Me you can do nothing."

God dwells in all of us, but there is a union that exceeds in dimension of reality all that we have ever experienced. It is a union of likeness. This union exists when God's will and the human soul are in conformity, so that nothing in the one is repugnant to the other. When the soul rids itself completely of what is hostile and contrary to the divine will, it then rests transformed in God through love.

Rom. 8:9b, NAS

If anyone does not have the Spirit of Christ, he does not belong to Him.

Gal. 5:17a, NAS

Flesh sets its desire against the Spirit, and the Spirit against the flesh.

Union cannot be accomplished unless there is similarity of substance. Flesh and spirit cannot be merged into one unifying substance. They cannot be merged together (as water and oil) because they are explicitly alien to one another.

For there to be union, the flesh must die at the cross. The new life that emerges must be exposed to the divine catalyst of the

Logos whereby it is gradually transformed into new expressions of "spirit."

> "There is a lot of teaching in the earth today about the Body of Christ...how God has sent forth His gifts upon His people to bind them together in a common fellowship, and to endue them with power and anointing that they might become vital members of the glorious Body of Christ. And yet, sad to say, there seems to be very little evidence in our assemblies of the mighty, abiding Presence of Christ, and of His Lordship in the lives of His people. I think that the reason is quite evident. We want His blessings and His gifts and His miracle working power, and we cry out for more and more of these...but He answers back: 'My desire is that you should come into total union with Myself, and walk in My truth, in My life, in My holiness, in My patience, in My longsuffering, in My kindness, in My mercy, in My love...I want you to be ONE WITH ME in all things.'"[2]

Suffering of the Overcomer

Rom. 8:17, NAS

and if children, heirs also, heirs of God and fellow heirs with Christ, if indeed we suffer with Him so that we may also be glorified with Him.

Heb 5:14, NAS

But solid food is for the mature, who because of practice have their senses trained to discern good and evil.

Heb 12:11, NAS

All discipline for the moment seems not to be joyful, but sorrowful; yet to those who have been trained by it, afterwards it yields the peaceful fruit of righteousness.

The womb is a secure place where all of our needs are met. We are cushioned from the blows of life and never experience a single worry. But the womb was never meant to be our home. It is a place of transition between the blackness of "nonexistence" and the brightness of "life." At some point, we begin to feel the pressure as we are slowly pushed out of that comfortable abode. Pressure, more than we have ever experienced before, is thrusting us out of our secure and soft environment. "What is going on?" we cry out. Pain is pressing in around us as we are delivered into the darkness of that cold, empty birth canal. We think that this is the end of our life. We cannot survive one more push of pain. We feel abandoned and alone. Who will deliver us? Somebody, please stop this pain.

Finally, we reach the end. We plunge into a new dimension of existence. We are lifted up by the Deliverer and are quickly startled by a thumping pain pounding on our flesh. We begin to experience a breath of life flooding into our newly formed lungs. We struggle as we gasp for air.

Life has begun.

Literally, thousands of people around the world are experiencing the pressure and pain of what we have just described. They have enjoyed the safety and security of their life in Christ. They have felt the power of His presence and the blessings of His life. These precious ones have poured out their very lives into the purposes of God.

One by one, though, they find that life has become dull. The grief of unfulfilled expectations and the trauma of relational stress have worn away at the fiber of their souls. For some, the pain of physical ailments has interrupted the activities of their lives. The disappointment of present church structures and an ache for something different has left them spiritually numb. They feel abandoned and alone, wondering why God has left them.

In the midst of this pain God is revealing His purposes and plans. His desire is not to abandon us but to bring us into a new dimension—into the dimension where He lives. There is only one way to get into that place. We must pass through the birth canal. We must go through the "dark night of the soul."

As we pass this way, we are stripped of the flesh and prepared to take on a glorious new life. Our pain is simply a part of the process that will lead us into the presence of the Lord.[3]

It is the training for sonship and the preparation to reign with him. Now is not the time to give up. Now is the time to let that life begin.

This new life begins with a song. It is a song that has been birthed in the sea of despair and pain. It is a new song whose melody is magnificent and whose words are full of wonder.

The tale of God's three sons rises to its crescendo in this final conclusion—each "son" has a song to sing...

The Song of Moses

Moses, God's first son, wrote the 90th Psalm. (Rabbinical tradition also ascribes Psalms 91-100 to his authorship.) This, the oldest of the all the Psalms, bears this inscription: A Prayer of Moses the man of God. Psalm 90 has been called the "Psalm of Man's Fallen Condition," emphasizing the eternity of God and the brevity of human life. Some have called Moses' psalm "The Song of God Our Help."

For a full, verse-by-verse exegesis of Psalm 90, see my book *Principles of Present Truth From Psalms 73-150* (Richlands, NC: Tabernacle Press, 1985).

The first son was chosen to deliver Israel from the tyranny of Egypt and its cruel ruler. Moses' triumph over Pharaoh and his army took place at the Red Sea, and is narrated in Exodus chapter 14. The following chapter records his song of celebration.

Exod 15:1-21, KJV

> *Then sang Moses and the children of Israel this song unto the Lord, and spake, saying, I will sing unto the Lord, for He hath triumphed gloriously* [to rise up and be exalted]*: the horse and his rider hath He thrown into the sea.*

The Lord is my strength and song, and He is become my salvation: He is my God, and I will prepare [prepare, adorn] *Him an habitation; my father's God, and I will exalt Him.*

The Lord is a man of war: the Lord is His name.

Pharaoh's chariots and his host hath He cast into the sea: his chosen captains also are drowned in the Red sea.

The depths have covered them: they sank into the bottom as a stone [like the hardness of Pharaoh's heart].

Thy right hand, O Lord, is become glorious in power: Thy right hand, O Lord, hath dashed in pieces the enemy.

And in the greatness of Thine excellency [majesty] *Thou hast overthrown them that rose up against Thee: Thou sentest forth Thy wrath, which consumed them as stubble.*

And with the blast [spirit] *of Thy nostrils the waters were gathered together, the floods stood upright as an heap, and the depths were congealed* [thickened, curdled] *in the heart of the sea.*

The enemy said, I will pursue, I will overtake, I will divide the spoil; my lust [soul's desire] *shall be satisfied upon them; I will draw my sword, my hand shall destroy them.*

Thou didst blow with Thy wind, the sea covered them: they sank as lead in the mighty waters.

Who is like unto Thee, O Lord, among the gods? who is like Thee, glorious in holiness, fearful in praises, doing wonders?

Thou stretchedst out Thy right hand, the earth swallowed them.

Thou in Thy mercy hast led forth the people which Thou hast redeemed: Thou hast guided them in Thy strength unto Thy holy habitation.

The people shall hear, and be afraid: sorrow [pain, anguish] *shall take hold on the inhabitants of Palestina.*

Then the dukes [chieftans] *of Edom shall be amazed; the mighty men of Moab, trembling shall take hold upon them; all the inhabitants of Canaan shall melt away.*

Fear and dread shall fall upon them; by the greatness of Thine arm [power] *they shall be as still as a stone; till Thy people pass over, O Lord, till the people pass over, which Thou hast purchased.*

Thou shalt bring them in, and plant them in the mountain of Thine inheritance [Mount Zion], *in the place, O Lord, which Thou hast made for Thee to dwell in, in the Sanctuary, O Lord, which Thy hands have established.*

The Lord shall reign for ever and ever.

For the horse of Pharaoh went in with his chariots and with his horsemen into the sea, and the Lord brought again the waters of the sea upon them; but the children of Israel went on dry land in the midst of the sea.

And Miriam the prophetess, the sister of Aaron, took a timbrel [tambourine] *in her hand; and all the women went out after her with timbrels and with dances.*

And Miriam answered them, Sing ye to the Lord, for He hath triumphed gloriously; the horse and his rider hath He thrown into the sea.

Micah 6:4, KJV

For I brought thee up out of the land of Egypt, and redeemed thee out of the house of servants; and I sent before thee Moses, Aaron, and Miriam.

Following their departure from Egypt, Moses and Israel were led forth in mercy, redeemed in grace, and guided by strength. Theirs was a new standing and position. The glorious crossing of the Red Sea was their God-given guarantee and pledge that Jehovah would finish the work that He had begun in His man and His people.

Exodus chapter 15 parallels Revelation chapter 15. The song of Moses, the first song recorded in Scripture, is also known as "The Song of Redemption." Israel's sighing gave way to singing, and their groaning to praising. This song of deliverance is God-centered, as the word *Lord* appears 12 times in its first 18 verses. The pronouns *He, Him, Thou, Thy,* and *Thee* are found over 30 times. This principle of praise is summed up in Exodus 15:2: "I will exalt Him."

The song of Moses ends in verse 18 as it begins in verse 1, with the sovereign "Lord." Although it is beyond the scope of this writing, it is significant that Moses would conclude his wilderness career with a second song (Deut. 32:1-47). God's first son learned how to sing!

The Song of Jesus

Each of God's three "sons" has a song. But of these three deliverers, Jesus alone is the exalted One. The quality of His song recalls one of David's captains, Adino, whose name means "chief of the three" (2 Sam. 23:8). Jesus' song is the chief song and He is the "chief singer" (Hab. 3:19). The song of the Pattern Son inspired the title of this final chapter, which illustrates this truth. My booklet, *Sing, O Barren* (Richlands, NC: Tabernacle Press, 1988), sets forth the seven barren women of Scripture:

1. Sarah was mother to the son of promise, Isaac (laughter and joy).

2. Rebekeh brought forth Jacob, who became Israel (transformation).

3. Rachel mothered the statesman, Joseph (humility and patience).

4. Manoah's wife brought forth the powerful judge, Samson (strength).

5. Hannah gave birth to Samuel (the spirit of prophecy).

6. Elisabeth bore John the Baptist (repentance and purging).

Ultimately, the virgin Mary, the seventh "barren" woman mentioned in the Bible, was chosen to give birth to Jesus—total perfection—from the epitome of "barrenness," her virgin womb!

The names "Mary" and "Miriam" come from the same Hebrew root, *marah*, which means, "bitter." Miriam's voice and timbrel echoed the song of Moses when they crossed the Red Sea and witnessed the downfall of Pharaoh's host. Paralleling this model is the triumphant Magnificat of Mary (Lk. 1:46-55), who sang and rejoiced at the birth of our Savior.

Lk. 1:41, KJV

And it came to pass, that, when Elisabeth heard the salutation of Mary, the babe leaped [skipped, jumped] *in her womb; and Elisabeth was filled with the Holy Ghost.*

The testimony of Jesus is the spirit of prophecy (Rev. 19:10). The words below are not just the words of Mary. The divine Seed Himself was singing in the midst of her! Mary's embrace of Elisabeth caused that which was prophetic yet unborn to leap. But in the Magnificat, Jesus, the Word made flesh, sang! Each of the verses of this song tells of Him, the living Word, who is the second Son, the Pattern Son.

"And Mary said, My soul doth magnify the Lord" (Lk. 1:46, KJV)—This bears witness to the size of God's Word. The word "magnify" means, "to make (or declare) great, increase or extol."

"And my spirit hath rejoiced in God my Saviour" (Lk. 1:47, KJV)—This shows the joy of God's Word. Mary "rejoiced" or "jumped for joy" at the thought of God her Savior!

"For He hath regarded the low estate of His handmaiden: for, behold, from henceforth all generations shall call me blessed" (Lk. 1:48, KJV)—This tells of the depth of God's Word. The word "regarded" means, "to gaze at with pity." "Low" means, "to be depressed or humiliated (in rank or feeling)." Compare the *kenosis* or "emptying" of Christ as set forth in Philippians 2:1-11.

"For He that is mighty hath done to me great things; and holy is His name" (Lk. 1:49, KJV)—This boasts of the might of God's Word. "Mighty" is *dunatos*, which means "powerful or capable," and speaks of the power of the Holy Spirit.

"And His mercy is on them that fear Him from generation to generation" (Lk. 1:50, KJV)—This reveals the mercy of God's Word. "Mercy" is "compassion," the outward manifestation of pity. Mercy assumes need on the part of him who receives it, and adequate resources to meet the need on the part of him who shows it.

"He hath showed strength with His arm; He hath scattered the proud [as Jehovah did with Pharaoh] in the imagination of their hearts" (Lk. 1:51, KJV)—This emphasizes the strength of God's Word. "Strength" is *kratos*, which means "force, manifested power."

"He hath put down the mighty from their seats, and exalted them [as Jehovah did with Moses] of low degree" (Lk. 1:52, KJV)—This displays the justice of God's Word. He has "put down" or "violently demolished" the mighty (dynasties) from their "seats" or "thrones," and "exalted" or "elevated" those of low estate.

"He hath filled the hungry with good things; and the rich He hath sent empty away" (Lk. 1:53, KJV)—This underscores the satisfaction of God's Word. Compare this verse with Job 23:12; Jeremiah 15:16; and Matthew 4:4; 5:6.

"He hath holpen His servant Israel, in remembrance of His mercy" (Lk. 1:54, KJV)—This narrates the support of God's Word. "Holpen" means, "to take hold of in turn, to succour."

"As He spake to our fathers, to Abraham, and to his seed for ever" (Lk. 1:55, KJV)—This bears witness to the faithfulness of

God's Word. God remembered His covenant with the patriarchal fathers—Abraham, Isaac, and Jacob.[4]

Hab. 3:19, KJV

...To the chief singer on my stringed instruments.

The prophet Habakkuk, himself a temple musician, foresaw Messiah as the "Chief Singer," or "Choir Director" (NAS). Jesus is the "Director or Music" (NIV), the "Choirmaster" (RSV).

Jesus is the Chief Singer. A similar phrase, "To the chief musician," is found in the inscriptions over exactly 50 (the biblical number denoting Pentecost, Jubilee, and the anointing) of the Psalms. The One who is the Chief Singer is further revealed in the New Testament as "the chief corner stone" (Eph. 2:20; 1 Pet. 2:6) and the "chief shepherd" (1 Pet. 5:4).

The Chief Singer is the Head of the Church. Jesus by His Spirit stands in the midst of us, individually and corporately, and sings! David bore witness to this as he was anointed by the same Messianic Spirit. Through the sweet psalmist of Israel, we hear the voice of Him who is the greatest Son of David, King of kings.

Psa 22:22, KJV

I will declare [enumerate, recount, celebrate] *Thy name unto My brethren: in the midst of the congregation will I praise Thee.*

Ps. 22:22, TLB

I will praise you to all My brothers; I will stand up before the congregation and testify of the wonderful things You have done.

We learned in an earlier chapter that the name or nature of God is the revelation of all that He is, all that He has, and all that He does. The awareness of His name forms the basis of the lyrics of the Song of the Lamb in the midst of us! The writer to the Hebrews bears witness to the song of the second Son.

Heb. 2:11-12, KJV

For both He that sanctifieth and they who are sancti-
fied are all [out of] *of one* [Father]: *for which cause He is*
not ashamed [disfigured or disgraced] *to call them*
brethren [family],

Saying, I will declare Thy name unto My brethren, in
the midst of the church will I sing praise unto Thee.

Heb. 2:12, TLB

For He says in the book of Psalms, "I will talk to My
brothers about God My Father, and together we will sing
His praises."

Jesus is always speaking—He is the eternal Word (Jn. 1:1).

Jesus is always praying—He ever lives to make intercession
for His people (Rom. 8:34; Heb. 7:25).

Jesus is always singing—let Him sing in the midst of you!

The Song of Moses and the Song of the Lamb

Every 2,000 years, God has a "son." Each son has a song.
Moses sang. Jesus sings. The third Son, the Manchild, the mature
Church, is blessed with the "double portion," the portion of the
firstborn (Deut. 21:17; 2 Kings 2:9). We are privileged to sing the
Song of Moses, *and* the Song of the Lamb!

Rev. 15:2-4, KJV

And I saw as it were a sea of glass mingled with fire:
and them that had gotten the victory over the beast, and
over his image, and over his mark, and over the number of
his name, stand on the sea of glass, having the harps of
God.

And they sing the song of Moses the servant of God,
and the song of the Lamb, saying, Great and marvellous
[wonderful] *are Thy works, Lord God Almighty; just and*
true are Thy ways, Thou King of saints.

Who shall not fear Thee, O Lord, and glorify Thy name? for Thou only art holy: for all nations shall come and worship before Thee; for Thy judgments are made manifest.

These verses in Revelation 15 describe the Overcomer as a corporate company of praisers who have "gotten the victory." This word is *nikao* (Strong's #3528) and it means, "to subdue; conquer, overcome, prevail; to carry off the victory." It is translated in the Book of Revelation (KJV) 13 times as "overcometh, overcame, overcome."

The Revelator sees these overcomers standing victoriously upon a "sea of glass mingled with fire." Whatever this experience is, it is under their feet! The "sea of glass" points back to the laver in the Tabernacle of Moses (Ex. 30:17-21; 38:8), and the molten sea in the Temple of Solomon (1 Kings 7:23-25; 2 Chron. 4:2-5)—both speak of baptism, washing, and cleansing.

That John's sea of glass was "mingled" or "mixed" with fire shows that this is a picture of the *third* baptism, the baptism of fire![5]

The first baptism is in water, and the second is in the Holy Ghost. But this third experience is in fire, prefigured by Israel's baptism into Joshua at the Jordan River when they crossed over into the land of promise (Josh. 3-4; 1 Cor. 10:1-4,11). This *third* baptism enables the Overcomer, the mature Church, to be delivered "over" or "out from":

1. The "beast" ("wild beast")—the old Adamic nature (Rom. 6:1-14).

2. The "image" ("likeness, profile, resemblance") of the beast—the world, and all that is in the world (1 Jn. 2:15-17).

3. The "mark" (*charagma*, the "character") of the beast—the idolatry of all human wisdom (the forehead) and human strength (the right hand) (Rev. 13:16). The overcomer is sealed, having received the "mark" of the Lord.[6]

4. The "number" ("something added up; multitude") of the beast—the full expression of man revealed in the number 666 (Rev. 13:17-18). This is pictured in King Solomon, the epitome of the natural man, as narrated in the Book of Ecclesiastes. Solomon was the man who knew it all, who had it all, and who did it all.[7]

Finally, Revelation 15:4 reveals that those who sing the Song of Moses and the Song of the Lamb are alive in the time when all nations shall come up to Zion to worship the King of saints. This is the Feast of Tabernacles, when His judgments (righteous acts) are being manifested (made visible) throughout the earth!

Chapter Four of this volume noted that the Manchild company of overcomers of Revelation 12 and the 144,000 of Revelation 14 are one and the same. The latter are seen standing with the prevailing Lamb on Mount Zion with His Father's name written in their foreheads. John declared that as they stood, they sang.

Rev. 14:2-3, TLB

And I heard a sound from heaven like the roaring of a great waterfall or the rolling of mighty thunder. It was the singing of a choir accompanied by harps.

This tremendous choir—144,000 strong—sang a wonderful new song in front of the throne of God and before the four Living Beings and the twenty-four Elders; and no one could sing this song except those 144,000 who had been redeemed from the earth.

The song of the 144,000 is the song of the third Son, the corporate Son, the voice of "many waters."[8] This is the "new song" for the dawning of this new day, the Third Day in God (Hos. 6:1-3).

The only ones who can "learn"[9] this new song are those who have followed the Lamb all the way into the throne room, the place of His full authority and lordship over their lives! The third Son, the overcoming, glorious Church, has been apprehended to sing the song of Moses *and* the Song of the Lamb!

Song 2:10-14, KJV

My beloved spake, and said unto me, Rise up, my love, my fair one, and come away.

For, lo, the winter is past, the rain is over and gone;

The flowers appear on the earth; the time of the singing of birds is come, and the voice of the turtle (turtle-dove) *is heard in our land;*

The fig tree putteth forth her green figs, and the vines with the tender grape give a good smell. Arise, my love, my fair one, and come away.

O my dove, that art in the clefts of the rock, in the secret places of the stairs, let me see thy countenance, let me hear thy voice; for sweet is thy voice, and thy countenance is comely.

Every 2,000 years, God has a "son"—Moses, Jesus, and the mature Church. Each of the three has a song. Once again in the earth, it is time to sing.

Arise and sing, O barren! Ascend with your praise! Break forth and cry aloud! Winter and tribulation are past (Mt. 24:20-21). Let Him hear your voice!

As you sing, remember the seven barren women of the Bible. Sarah, the mother of Isaac, has come out of her tent. Laughter is the heir of God.

Rebekah, the mother of Jacob (who became Israel) has jumped off her camel. The sun has arisen upon Peniel, and upon the place and face of transformation.

Rachel, the mother of Joseph, has done away with her teraphim (household idols). A spirit of patience and humility is being unveiled to the other brethren.

Manoah's wife, the mother of Samson, is speaking up. God's strength is about to bring down the house of the Philistines.

Hannah, the mother of Samuel, is rejoicing. Her sigh has become a song. Once again, the voice of a real prophet is heard in the land.

Something is leaping in the womb of Elisabeth, the mother of John the Baptist. Repentance and purging are gathering quite a crowd on the banks of another baptism.

Mary, the mother of Jesus, has believed and received the impossible!

The One who completes and fulfills all things is coming forth in all glory and splendor! He has come, He is coming, and He shall come. Arise, O barren! Sing to your King!

Is. 54:1-3, KJV

> _Sing, O barren, thou that didst not bear; break forth into singing, and cry aloud, thou that didst not travail with child: for more are the children of the desolate than the children of the married wife, saith the Lord._

> _Enlarge the place of thy tent, and let them stretch forth the curtains of thine habitations: spare not, lengthen thy cords, and strengthen thy stakes;_

> _For thou shalt break forth on the right hand and on the left; and thy seed shall inherit the Gentiles_ [nations]...

It is evident that these opening verses from Isaiah 54 have to do with our prayer, our praise, and our worship—our song. This new song will produce a fivefold fruit that will empower us to inherit the nations:

1. Enlargement—"enlarge" ("broaden, make wide").

2. Stretching—"stretch forth" ("spread out, extend").

3. Boldness—"spare not" ("do not refrain, restrain, or refuse").

4. Lengthening—"lengthen" ("make long, prolong").

5. Strengthening—"strengthen" ("help, repair, fortify, sustain").

These five words, taken from Isaiah 54:2 (KJV), respectively prophesy that God's third corporate Son, the mature Church, will:

1. Be free of all prejudice, having widened their mercy.

2. Go where no other people have gone in the Holy Ghost.

3. Be radically bold, having been freed from the spirit of fear.

4. Be generational in their purpose, motive, and method.

5. Be the people who will "build the old waste places" and "raise up the foundations of many generations"; they shall be called the "repairer of the breach" and the "restorer of paths to dwell in" (Is. 58:12, KJV).

The Twenty-first Century—New Territory

Josh. 3:1-5, KJV

And Joshua rose early in the morning; and they removed from Shittim, and came to Jordan, he and all the children of Israel, and lodged there before they passed over.

And it came to pass after three days, that the officers went through the host;

And they commanded the people, saying, When ye see the ark of the covenant of the Lord your God, and the priests the Levites bearing it, then ye shall remove from your place, and go after it.

Yet there shall be a space between you and it, about two thousand cubits by measure: come not near unto it, that ye may know the way by which ye must go: for ye have not passed this way heretofore.

And Joshua said unto the people, Sanctify yourselves: for to morrow the Lord will do wonders among you.

The Ark of the Covenant in these verses is another important picture of Jesus. The piercing and dividing of the Jordan's waters by the Ark in Joshua's day prefigures the rending of the veil by our Savior and King. Two thousand cubits later, the Old Testament nation crossed the river, entered the land of promise, and began their conquest.

Two thousand years ago, our Savior and King finished His work at the cross. Now, two thousand years later, His holy nation, the glorious Church—the third Son, His seed, His brethren—follow their Leader, their Forerunner, into the Most Holy Place and the fullness of God (Heb. 6:19-20; 1 Pet. 2:9).

The 21st century Church has entered new territory—we have not passed this way before!

Rejoice, child of God. We have nothing to fear.

Just ask Moses. Pharaoh's army is drowned!

Ask Jesus, and Joseph, and Mary. Herod the Great is dead!

Ask the Overcomer. The ancient serpent that became a dragon has been totally defeated!

The Son, the Seed, is safe. The end is secure (Ps. 138:8; Jer. 29:11; Phil. 1:6).

Luke 1:34-37, KJV

Then said Mary unto the angel, How shall this be, seeing I know not a man?

And the angel answered and said unto her, The Holy Ghost shall come upon thee, and the power of the Highest shall overshadow thee: therefore also that holy thing which shall be born of thee shall be called the Son of God.

And, behold, thy cousin Elisabeth, she hath also conceived a son in her old age: and this is the sixth month with her, who was called barren.

For with God nothing shall be impossible.

Like Mary, we carry the divine Seed, the purpose and destiny of God. All we need is the Holy Ghost and Elisabeth. The Holy Spirit enables and empowers us from within. Our covenant brothers and sisters encourage and embrace us from without!

We can do all things through Christ, the One who personally enables us, and the One who embraces us through His corporate, covenant people. Nothing is impossible. No Word from God is void of power.

All we have now is His promise! All we can do now is sing!

Josh. 3:5, NIV

"Consecrate yourselves, for tomorrow the Lord will do amazing things among you."

The year 2000 has come and gone. The 21st century has dawned...

You who have been impregnated with the living Word, you who bear the prophetic burden of the Lord, sanctify yourselves as you cross the river...

Brothers and sisters, the Lord is about to do wonders among us!

Endnotes

Introduction

1. See Is. 13:1; 15:1; 17:1; 19:1; 21:1; 22:1; 23:1; Jer. 23:33-38; Nah. 1:1; Hab. 1:1; Zech. 9:1; 12:1.

Chapter One

1. Jn. 1:17; Gal. 3:19.

2. See Deut. 18:15; Acts 3:22-23; 4:12; 1 Tim. 2:5; Heb. 1:1-3.

3. See Rom. 8:17; 2 Cor. 5:17-21; Gal. 3:29; 4:1-7,28-30.

4. Jer. 3:14; Jn. 4:22; Gal. 4:4-5.

5. See Eph. 5:22-33; Rev. 2:7,11,17,26; 3:5,12,21; 12:1-5; 14:1-5.

6. Eph. 1:3; Phil. 4:19; 2 Pet. 1:3.

7. Prov. 13:22; Is. 60:1-5; Rev. 21:24.

8. Jn. 1:29; Eph. 4:8-10.

9. Rom. 8:29; compare Ps. 89:27; Jn. 17:16-26; 1 Cor. 15:49; 2 Cor. 3:18; Heb. 2:6-13; and 1 Jn. 3:1-3. Just as the golden lampstand in the Old Testament Tabernacle was beaten out of one piece of pure gold (Ex. 25:36), so Jesus and His brethren, He who sanctifies and they who are sanctified, are all "[out] of one" (Heb. 2:11), are all from one Father. This Greek expression is an ablative of source. Similarly, the root Greek word for "brethren" is *adelphos*, and it means "out of the womb, a womb-brother." The Psalmist called this spiritual womb "the womb of the morning" (Ps. 110:3), "the womb of the dawn" (NAS, NIV).

Chapter Two

1. Ps. 105:26; 106:23.
2. Compare Acts 7:17-37.
3. Ex. 2:11-15; Acts 7:23-28; compare Acts 8:3; 9:1-4; Phil. 3:1-9.
4. Ex. 4:2,4,17,20; 7:1.
5. See Num. 12:13-15; 16:20-22; 21:7; Deut. 33:6-17.
6. Num. 11:24-25; compare 1 Cor. 12:12; Gal. 4:6,19; Col. 1:27.
7. See Gen. 10:6; Ex. 1-12; 1 Chron. 1:8,11; Jn. 1:29; 1 Cor. 5:5-8; Eph. 2:1-3; 1 Jn. 2:15-17.
8. See Ex. 4:21; 14:4,17; Deut. 2:30; Josh. 11:19-20; 1 Sam. 6:6; Ps. 105:25; Rom. 9:18.
9. See Ex. 8:19; 31:18; Deut. 9:10; Lk. 11:20.
10. See Ex. 12:1-51; 34:25; Lev. 23:5; Num. 9:1-14; 28:16; 33:3; Deut. 16:1-8; Josh. 5:10-11; 2 Kings 23:21-23; 2 Chron. 30:1-18; 35:1-19; Ezra 6:19-20; Ezek. 45:21.
11. Concerning Israel's overnight abundance of blessing and wealth, see also Ex. 11:2; Ps. 68:11-13; 78:52; 136:11; Jer. 31:2; 32:21.
12. Compare Ps. 41:3-4; 103:3; 147:3; Is. 33:24; Jer. 8:22; 33:6; Hos. 6:1; 11:3.

Chapter Three

1. Both Testaments tell of His incarnation, the "mystery of godliness," how that "God was manifest in the flesh" (1 Tim. 3:16). In the Old Testament, see Gen. 3:15; Ps. 40:7; Is. 7:14; 9:6; Ezek. 3:15; and Mic. 5:2. In the New Testament, study Lk. 24:39; Jn. 1:14; Acts 2:30; Rom. 1:3; 8:3; 9:5; Gal. 4:4; Phil. 2:8; Col. 1:15; Heb. 1:3; 2:14,17; 4:15; 1 Jn. 1:2; 4:2-3; 2 Jn. 1:7; and Rev. 22:16.
2. Is. 42:1. As the "chosen" of God, Jesus was prefigured by King David in Psalm 89:3. Compare the usage of this word in 1 Chron. 16:13; Ps.105:6,43; 106:5,23; and Is. 43:20; 45:4; 65:9.
3. Heb. 4:15; compare Is. 53:4-5; Zech. 9:9; Lk. 4:1-14; 22:28; Rom. 8:3; 2 Cor. 5:21; 8:9; Phil. 2:5-11; Heb. 2:9-18; 5:2; 7:26; 1 Pet. 2:22; 1 Jn. 3:5.
4. Num. 11:24-25 with Mk. 14:36; Rom. 8:15; 1 Cor. 12:12; Gal. 4:6; Col. 1:27.
5. The wild man Esau ("rough, hairy"), the man of the field or the world, pictures the flesh. See Gen. 25:25-34; 26:34-35; 28:6-10; 36:1-8,43; Obad. 1; Mal. 1:2-3; Rom. 9:13; Heb. 12:16-17.
6. Herod the Great had a passion for pretentious display in magnificent architecture and monuments, as had all his ruling descendants after him.

To conciliate the Jews, who had been alienated by his cruelties, he proposed to reconstruct their ancient Temple that Solomon had originally built. It has been shrewdly suspected that he secretly entertained the sinister motive to possess himself of the public genealogies collected there, especially those relating to the priestly families. It is said by some that he thereby hoped to destroy the genealogy of the expected Messiah, lest He should come and usurp Herod's kingdom.

7. See 2 Sam. 8:2; Ps. 89:39,44; Is. 25:12; Lam. 5:16; 2 Cor. 10:5.

8. See Rom. 8:5-8; 1 Cor. 3:1-4; Eph. 4:18-19; Col. 1:21; 2 Thess. 2:3-4; 2 Tim. 3:4.

9. Hosea 11:1; see also Ex. 4:22-23; Num. 24:8; Acts 2:10.

10. See Jn. 15:19; Rom. 12:2; Gal. 5:13; Eph. 2:2; Col. 3:1-3; Jas. 4:4; 1 Pet. 2:9; 1 Jn. 2:15-17.

11. See Jn. 1:18; 3:16; Eph. 1:4; Tit. 1:2; 1 Pet. 1:18-20; Rev. 13:8; 17:8.

12. 2 Pet. 3:8 with Is. 53:2; Ezek. 17:22; Mt. 16:21; Mk. 14:12; Lk. 1:78; 20:15; 22:7; Jn. 12:24; Acts 3:15; 1 Thess. 2:15. Jesus was the Lamb without blemish (Ex. 12:5 with Is. 53:9; Lk 1:35; 23:41,47; Jn. 14:30; 2 Cor. 5:21; Heb. 4:15; 7:26; 9:14; 1 Pet. 1:19; 1 Jn. 3:5).

13. See Lev. 14:1-7; Ps. 51:7; Is. 52:15; 63:3; Ezek. 43:18; Jn. 19:29; Heb. 8:10; 9:13-14,19-21; 10:22; 11:28; 12:24; 1 Pet. 1:2.

14. See Ps. 34:20; 69:9; Is. 9:7; Jn. 19:36; Rom. 1:16-17; 2 Cor. 7:7; Gal. 6:14; Eph. 2:19-22; Phil. 2:5; 1 Pet. 2:21; Rev. 7:9-10.

15. See Mt. 20:22; 26:27,39,42; Lk. 22:1,7,17-20; Jn. 6:35-51; 8:46; 1 Cor. 5:6-8; 10:16; 11:25-28; 2 Cor. 5:21; Heb. 4:15; 7:26.

16. Jesus' girdle is revealed in Lev. 8:7; Ps. 65:6; 93:1; Is. 11:5; Dan. 10:5; Jn. 13:4-5; and Rev. 1:13. His shoes are mentioned in Deut. 33:25; Ruth 4:7-8; Mt. 3:11; Mk. 1:7; Lk. 3:16; 15:22; Jn. 1:27; and Acts 13:25. His staff (rod or scepter) is described in Gen. 49:10; Ex. 4:20; Num. 17:8; 24:17; Esther 4:11; 5:2; Ps. 2:9; 23:4; 45:6; 110:2; Is. 11:1; Heb. 1:8; 9:4; and Rev. 19:15.

17. See Ps. 2:7; 110:4; Jn. 4:34; 5:30; 6:38; 8:29; Heb. 5:8-9; 10:6-10; 13:20.

18. See Ex. 12:10; Ps. 16:10; Jon. 2:6; Acts 2:27-31; 13:34-37.

19. See Ex. 30:6; 36:35; 40:3; Lev. 16:2,12; Num. 4:5; 2 Chron. 3:14; Mk. 15:38; Lk. 23:45; Heb. 6:19; 9:3; 10:20. When Jesus died on Calvary and rent the veil, He led captivity captive (Judg. 5:12; Ps. 68:8; Eph. 4:8). "He led captives in His train" (NIV). The captives were not the redeemed, but the enemies of Christ's kingdom—satan, sin, and death (compare Is. 49:24-25; 53:12; Mt. 12:29; Lk. 11:22; Jn. 12:31; 16:11; Rom. 8:37; 1 Cor. 15:57; 2 Cor. 2:14; Col. 2:15; Heb. 2:14; Rev. 12:9; 20:2-3).

20. See Mic. 1:15; Mt. 21:38; Mk. 12:7; Lk. 20:14; Rom. 4:13; Gal. 4:1-7,30; Heb. 11:7.

21. Study these promises that God made to the "fathers"—Abraham, Isaac, and Jacob—in Genesis, chapters 12, 13, 15, 17, 22, 26, and 35.

22. For an understanding of the "all things" provided us in Christ, study Mt. 11:27; 19:26; 21:22; 22:4; 28:20; Jn. 1:3; 3:35; 13:3; 14:26; 15:15; 16:15; Acts 3:21; Rom. 11:36; 1 Cor. 2:10; 3:21; 8:6; 13:7; 2 Cor. 5:17; 6:10; 9:8; Eph. 1:10-11,22; 4:10,15; 5:20; Col. 1:16-20; 1 Tim. 6:13; 2 Tim. 2:7; Heb. 1:3; 2:8-10; 1 Jn. 2:20,27; Rev. 4:11; 21:5-7.

23. See Mt. 1:21-23; Acts 4:12; 15:26; 16:31; 1 Cor. 15:57; Gal. 6:14; Phil. 2:9; Rev. 22:21.

24. For the *El* names (Gen. 15:2), see these verses: *Elohim* (Gen. 1:1); *El-Shaddai* (Gen. 17:1); and *El-Elyon* (Gen. 14:18-19).

25. For the ten *Jehovah* compound names (Ex. 3:14-15) as they appear in scriptural order, see Gen. 22:14; Ex. 15:26; 17:15; 31:13; Judg. 6:24; 11:27; Ps. 23:1; 95:6; Jer. 23:6; and Ezek. 48:35.

Chapter Four

1. See Gal. 4:21-31; Eph. 1:3,20-23; 2:6; 3:10; 5:22-33; Heb. 12:22-24; Rev. 3:12; 21:12.

2. Zion was the capital city of David, the center of all kingly government and priestly function (see 2 Sam. 5:7; 1 Kings 8:1; Ps. 2:6; 48:1-2; 76:2; 102:13-16; 132:13; Is. 2:3; 4:5-6; 52:7-8; 66:8; Jer. 3:14; Joel 2:23,32; 3:16-21; Mic. 4:2; Zech. 1:17; 9:9,13). With regard to Sion in the New Testament, compare Mt. 21:5; Jn. 12:15; Rom. 9:33; 11:26; Heb. 12:22; 1 Pet. 2:6.

3. See Ps. 29:3; Ezek. 1:24; 43:2; Rev. 1:15; 19:6.

4. See Ps. 33:3; 40:3; 96:1; 98:1; 144:9; 149:1; Is. 42:10; Rev. 5:9.

5. See Gen. 49:19; Num. 13:30; Lk. 10:19; 11:22; Jn. 16:33; Rom. 8:37; 12:21; 16:20; 1 Jn. 2:13-14; 4:4; 5:4; Rev. 2:7,11,17,26; 3:5,12,21; 17:14; 21:7.

6. See Rev. 12:3-4,7,9,13,16-17; 13:2, 4,11; 16:13; 20:2.

7. For Michael, the warring archangel, see Dan. 10:13,21; 12:1; Jude 1:9.

8. The word "ready" is mentioned throughout both Testaments (see Ex. 19:11; 34:2; 1 Kings 6:7; 1 Chron. 28:2; Ezra 7:6; Ps. 45:1; Mt. 22:1-8; 24:44; 25:10; Mk. 14:38; Lk. 1:17; Jn. 7:6; Acts 21:13; Rom. 1:15; 2 Cor. 8:19; 1 Tim. 6:18; 2 Tim. 4:6; Tit. 3:1; 1 Pet. 3:15; 5:2; Rev. 19:7).

9. Geoffrey Bull, *The Sky Is Red* (London: Hodder & Stoughton, 1965), p. 146.

10. See Deut. 12:2; 1 Kings 14:23; 2 Kings 16:4; 17:10; 2 Chron. 28:4; Job 15:32; Ps. 37:35; 52:8; Song 1:16; Is. 57:5; Jer. 2:20; 3:6,13; 11:16; 17:2,8; Ezek. 6:13; Hos. 14:8.

11. See Ex. 19:11-16; Hos. 6:1-3; Lk. 13:32; Jn. 2:1.

12. See Rom. 6:4; 1 Cor. 13:10-11; 2 Cor. 4:16; 5:17; Eph. 2:15; 4:3,13; Col. 3:10.

13. Concerning Messiah's "seed," see Gen. 3:15; Ps. 22:30; Is. 6:13; 53:2,10; Mt. 1:1; Rom. 8:29; Gal. 3:16,29; 4:6,19; Col. 1:27; Heb. 2:6-13; 1 Pet. 1:23. In Matthew 1:1-17, we count actually but 41 generations. The missing one, the 42nd, is found in the phrase "unto Christ" in verse 17—Jesus Christ is the 41st generation, and Christ the Body is the 42nd!

14. See Ps. 89:32; Prov. 10:13; 13:24; 22:15; 23:14; 26:3; 29:15; Lam. 3:1.

15. For an in-depth study about this corporate "branch" of the Lord, see Ps. 80:14-15; Prov. 9:1 (with 2 Kings 11:14) and 11:28; Is. 4:1-6; Jer. 23:5-6; 33:14-16; Zech. 4:11-14 and 6:12-13 (with 1 Chron. 22:5-6 and Rev. 2:26-29; 3:21; 21:7); Jn. 15:1-5.

Chapter Five

1. Unless otherwise noted, the material in the section "Secrets of Union" was graciously provided by Don Milam. I use it here with his permission.

2. George Warnock, *The Refiner's Fire: The Call to Intimate Relationship* (Dixon, MO: Rare Christian Books, n.d.), p. 54.

3. Material in the section "Suffering of the Overcomer" to this point is used by permission of Don Milam.

4. Jesus Christ "confirmed" or "secured" the promises made to the "fathers"—Abraham, Isaac, and Jacob (Acts 3:13). See Gen. 12:3; 17:19; 22:18; 26:4; 28:14.

5. See Mt. 3:11; 20:22-23; Lk. 3:16; Heb. 12:29.

6. The Greek word translated seven times (KJV) in the Book of Revelation as "mark" is the word *charagma* (Strong's #5480), and it means "a scratch or etching, i.e. stamp (as a badge of servitude), or sculptured figure (statue)." Thayer's Lexicon adds that *charagma* means "an imprinted mark; the mark branded upon horses; a thing carved, a sculpture, a graven work; used of idolatrous images." Vine's Dictionary adds that *charagma* is from *charasso* ("to engrave"), and kin to *charakter* (English, "character"), which means "the exact expression (the image) of any person or anything, marked likeness, precise reproduction in every respect, that is, facsimile." *Charagma* is found one other place in the New Testament; in Acts 17:29 it is translated as "graven" (KJV). The "mark" of the "beast" (Adam) is a present reality. See Ezek. 9:4; Rev. 3:12; 7:3-4; 13:16-17; 14:1,9,11; 16:2; 19:20; 20:4.

7. See Gen. 6:5; 1 Kings 10:14; Ps. 39:5; Eccles. 1–2.

8. "Waters" represent humanity. These "many waters" are the voice of God expressed through the corporate voice of a "new" (regenerated)

humanity—the one new Man (see Num. 24:7; 2 Sam. 22:17; Ps. 18:16; 29:3; Jer. 51:13; Ezek. 43:2; Rev. 1:15; 14:2; 19:6.

9. The word for "learn" in Revelation 14:3 is *manthano* (Strong's #3129), and it means, "to understand." Thayer's Lexicon adds that *manthano* means "to increase one's knowledge; to hear, to be informed; to learn by use and practice, to be in the habit of, accustomed to." Vine's Dictionary notes that *manthano* is akin to *mathetes* ("a disciple"), and means "to learn by inquiry, or observation." This word is used 31 times in the New Testament, including Mt. 11:29; Jn. 6:45; Rom. 16:17; 1 Cor. 14:31; Eph. 4:20; Phil. 4:9,11; 2 Tim. 3:14.

Appendix A

This is the prophetic utterance that flowed through Clarice Fluitt at Praise Tabernacle on Sunday morning, February 18, 2001, with regard to *Moses, the Master, and the Manchild.*

"You words, you words, you disciples taught of the Lord, you servants of the Most High God, I command you to issue forth out of Zion to do the bidding of God. To the north and south and east and west, listen, words, we call you blessed. Now go do what you must do. Go do what you must do...

"Release the prisoners that have been in the bondage of their mind. Release the revelation that the blood of God has made His Body divine. Release the revelation of a corporate Man. Release, you words, written on paper that once was wood. Go do the things that you know that you should. Words...the Kingdom of God is a Kingdom of words. And, surely as Jesus, the Word made flesh, in this day...not a mystery anymore, not a mystery anymore. It has been given to you and me to see the corporate Man, the destiny. Let these words in this book...let the devil take a good look, and know that we know that he is old and ugly and defeated, having no glorified body, having no power except that which we have erroneously given him because of false doctrine.

"Go, as the antidote to the antichrist to the nations of the world. Let it be so obviously God that no flesh could glory. Go, as a purifying influence that, Lord, blind eyes will be opened, deaf ears will begin to hear,

"'Oh, my God, it is no longer I who live, but Christ that lives. And no longer will I see male or female, or black or white, or yellow or red. The only thing that I will see...to as many as received Him, to them He gave the power to become the sons of God.'

"Stretch your hands toward these ordinary things that become extraordinary, because we who are the flesh made into the Word, we are arising out of the phoenix, the ashes of religious traditions of the mind of man. And we are coming forth, not with requests, but only command, placing pressure in the heavenlies, speaking to this book.

"Listen, O ye earth, take another look. We are coming out of Zion, saviors out of the womb of the morning, the breaking of a new day.

"We speak to these words that go say what Jesus has to say. We bind and break those that would take these words apart from the spirit in which they were written. We say right now, when it goes to press, anything that would want to attach itself to it that is not of God is smitten...no problems. We call it paid for. We call it paid for. We call it paid for.

"Father, we pray that this would be the most powerful book that Kelley has ever written. It will be written and read as no other book that has come forth from his hand. Lord, let this be the breaking of a Third Day, a glorious, victorious, corporate Man. The walls of prejudice, not just coming down, but that the sons of God rising above them, refusing, just simply realizing, 'I'm bigger than that, and we just step right over.'

"And all the church said, 'Amen!'"

Books & Tapes by Kelley Varner

Tape Catalog

To receive a full listing of Pastor Varner's books and tapes (audio and video), or information about our Tape of the Month and Seminars and Conferences, write or call for our current catalog:

Praise Tabernacle
P.O. Box 785
Richlands, NC 28574-0785
Phone: (910) 324-5026 or 324-5027
FAX: (910) 324-1048
E-mail: kvarner@nternet.net OR
            kvarner@templebuilders.com

Internet: www.kelleyvarner.com OR
          www.templebuilders.com

E-mail Newsletter

Subscribe to Pastor Varner's weekly e-mail newsletter, "The Praise Report," a resource for leaders, at www.kelleyvarner.com

Tape of the Month

Two cassette tapes (including sermon notes), by Pastor Varner and other ministries, are available each month on a monthly or annual offering basis. Write or call to join this growing family of listeners.

Conferences and Seminars

A variety of gatherings happen throughout the year here at Praise Tabernacle and the Crystal Coast Conference Center. Pastor Varner and the ministry team at Praise Tabernacle are also available for ministry in your church and local area.

Exciting titles
by Kelley Varner

━━ PREVAIL—A HANDBOOK FOR THE OVERCOMER

Pastor Varner believes that the key principle to moving on in God is a balance of two extremes. You must have both a solid foundation in biblical principles and a knowledge of how to make them practical in your life. Here you'll learn three basic ways to be an overcomer.
ISBN 0-938612-06-9

━━ THE MORE EXCELLENT MINISTRY

This is a book for those seeking greater fulfillment in their fellowship with the Lord and genuine, consistent power in their ministry. There is a more excellent way at the threshold of the Most Holy Place where His fullness flows unhindered. This place is reserved for people who want Him, no matter the price.
ISBN 0-914903-60-8

━━ THE PRIESTHOOD IS CHANGING

Pastor Varner deals with the practical dynamics of growing up in the Lord, moving from adolescence to maturity, from double-mindedness to confidence, from the Holy Place to the Most Holy Place. He speaks of a glorious return to the centrality and preeminence of Jesus Christ in our daily lives.
ISBN 1-56043-033-8

Are you committed to growing in God? Are you seeking greater fulfillment in your relationship with Him? Don't miss any one of these three books! Their message can change your life!

━━ UNDERSTANDING TYPES, SHADOWS & NAMES, VOLS. 1 & 2

The first two volumes in a series, they examine the main definition of a biblical term, its themes, how Christ fulfilled it, and how it applies to Christianity.
Vol. 1 ISBN 1-56043-165-2   Vol. 2 ISBN 1-56043-197-0

━━ WHOSE RIGHT IT IS

Here Pastor Varner carefully examines the Scriptures for a proper perspective on Christ's Lordship and dispensationalism.
ISBN 1-56043-151-2

━━ REST IN THE DAY OF TROUBLE

This book studies in detail the prophecy of Habakkuk. We too are in a day of trouble and, like Habakkuk, can we find rest in ours?
ISBN 1-56043-119-9

━━ CORPORATE ANOINTING

Just as a united front is more powerful in battle, so is the anointing when Christians come together in unity! Learn how God longs to reveal the fullness of Christ in the fullness of His Body in power and glory.
ISBN 0-7684-2011-3

━━ THE THREE PREJUDICES

Three walls of prejudice are still blocking God's power from flowing freely and as strongly as He desires. Our fear of rejection and misconceptions build these walls between us and our fellow believers. Learn the truth from the Bible about gender, race, and nations!
ISBN 1-56043-187-3

━━ UNSHAKEABLE PEACE

In a detailed study of the Book of Haggai, Pastor Varner presents the *unshakeable peace* that characterizes the Church that Jesus is building!
ISBN 1-56043-137-7

━━ THE TIME OF THE MESSIAH

There are four characteristics of the Messiah's first coming. Can you recognize these same signs in our present season—the season of the Holy Spirit upon the Church?
ISBN 1-56043-177-6

Available at your local Christian bookstore.

For more information and sample chapters, visit www.reapernet.com

Exciting titles
by Don Nori

━━━ NO MORE SOUR GRAPES

Who among us wants our children to be free from the struggles we have had to bear? Who among us wants the lives of our children to be full of victory and love for their Lord? Who among us wants the hard-earned lessons from our lives given freely to our children? All these are not only possible, they are also God's will. You can be one of those who share the excitement and joy of seeing your children step into the destiny God has for them. If you answered "yes" to these questions, the pages of this book are full of hope and help for you and others just like you.
ISBN 0-7684-2037-7

━━━ THE POWER OF BROKENNESS

Accepting Brokenness is a must for becoming a true vessel of the Lord, and is a stepping-stone to revival in our hearts, our homes, and our churches. Brokenness alone brings us to the wonderful revelation of how deep and great our Lord's mercy really is. Join this companion who leads us through the darkest of nights. Discover the *Power of Brokenness*.
ISBN 1-56043-178-4

━━━ THE ANGEL AND THE JUDGMENT

Few understand the power of our judgments—or the aftermath of the words we speak in thoughtless, emotional pain. In this powerful story about a preacher and an angel, you'll see how the heavens respond and how the earth is changed by the words we utter in secret.
ISBN 1-56043-154-7

━━━ HIS MANIFEST PRESENCE

This is a passionate look at God's desire for a people with whom He can have intimate fellowship. Not simply a book on worship, it faces our triumphs as well as our sorrows in relation to God's plan for a dwelling place that is splendid in holiness and love.
ISBN 0-914903-48-9
Also available in Spanish.
ISBN 1-56043-079-6

━━━ SECRETS OF THE MOST HOLY PLACE

Here is a prophetic parable you will read again and again. The winds of God are blowing, drawing you to His Life within the Veil of the Most Holy Place. There you begin to see as you experience a depth of relationship your heart has yearned for. This book is a living, dynamic experience with God!
ISBN 1-56043-076-1

━━━ HOW TO FIND GOD'S LOVE

Here is a heartwarming story about three people who tell their stories of tragedy, fear, and disease, and how God showed them His love in a real way.
ISBN 0-914903-28-4
Also available in Spanish.
ISBN 1-56043-024-9

Available at your local Christian bookstore.

For more information and sample chapters, visit www.reapernet.com